SAINT SIMON SAYS

MEMOIRS OF A REFORMED CATHOLIC SCHOOLBOY

SAINT SIMON SAYS

MEMOIRS OF A REFORMED CATHOLIC SCHOOLBOY

C.W. EMGE

2019

First Printing: 2019
ISBN: 978-0-578-57302-1

Author's note: The events described in these essays are real.
All characters have fictitious names and identifying characteristics.

Cover design / art direction by C.W. Emge.
Cover image licensed through Shutterstock.com.

This book was self-published.
Thank you for supporting independent authors and artists.

www.cwemge.com

For my father
and the words he could never find.

Good game, dad.

The Things We Refuse to Name

A painted rock, catfish from the grocery,
Your voice down the hall
A tornado through my trailer park.
My body's grown big
But my hands still feel so small.

I slipped into your shoes when you weren't looking.
The brown leather was still polished
And smelled like Sunday mornings.
They swallowed me to the ankle instantly
As I danced in your shadow.

A crack of light at the top of the stairs,
The jangling of keys,
The low rumble of Johnny Cash drifting from the radio,
The stash of sardines behind the bar,
All our secrets for the keeping.

These things we refuse to name,
The time we don't measure,
The words too slippery for our tongues,
I'll keep them here for you
In case you need them when I'm older.

"You perceive, now, that these things are all impossible except in a dream. You perceive that they are pure and puerile insanities, the silly creations of an imagination that is not conscious of its freaks—in a word, that they are a dream, and you the maker of it. The dream-marks are all present; you should have recognized them earlier."

— Mark Twain, *The Mysterious Stranger*

CONTENTS

JUNK DRAWER SPIRITUALITY

My grandmother was what I would call an everyday saint. She was a master of mundane miracles. And while she might not have been able to keep the party going by turning water into wine, she could somehow make my sore throat go away with little more than a glass of water and a few pinches of salt. That's some pretty powerful stuff to a skeptical eight-year-old and time and time again she made me a believer in her own special kind of magic.

She was also deeply, devoutly Catholic. Her faith, and the subsequent glow of grace that always seemed to surround her, was contagious in all the best ways. She was never much for quoting scripture other than an occasional reference to "the Good Book" and I don't remember much talk of sin, eternal damnation or anything even hinting of fire or brimstone. But she seemed to know all her saints by memory, including their holy day and what odd cause or industry they were the patron of—which is saying something considering the church currently recognizes somewhere around 2,550 saints. It's a pretty deep bench.

She didn't just "practice" her beliefs, though. They were deep in her bones, part of her spiritual DNA. And that faith always seemed to be expressed in simple-yet-super-real ways: Make sure everyone around you has enough on their plate before you sit down to eat. It takes more effort to be mean than it does to be kind, so you might as well be kind. Say you're sorry when you mess up and mean it. You are special and worthy of love—and so is everyone you meet.

Then there was my grandfather. I don't have the slightest idea how deep his knowledge of the saints was or his thoughts on any of the specifics of the religion. But I know he adored his wife and if something was important to her, it was important to him. I get the feeling faith was one of the many areas in his life where he followed his partner's lead. "Your grandma's in charge of stuff like that."

I do know he could recite that year's Cubs roster in a heartbeat. For someone who grew up and spent his entire life in St. Louis, that was considered high treason by his friends and neighbors. The ongoing feud between the Cards and Cubs is one of the more heated rivalries in baseball, more akin to the Hatfields & McCoys than a simple bi-state squabble.

My grandfather couldn't care less. He was second-generation

Irish American and as stubborn as a mule. He grew up a big St. Louis Browns fan, back before they packed their bags and headed to Baltimore to become the seasonally-underwhelming Orioles. He refused to cheer for the "other" St. Louis team and in what I can now see as a brilliant, if not hyper-personal rebellion, he decided to follow the Cubs feverishly year after year.

He also insisted on wearing buttoned-up, long-sleeve flannel shirts in the heart of summer for whatever that's worth.

I like to think I inherited a bit of that hard-headed "screw 'em all if they don't like it" attitude, if only mildly tempered by my grandmother's innate softness for the world around her. The end result being my sometimes overly-aggressive isolationism confusingly paired with genuine concern for and interest in other people. So for me, the sentiment has always felt a little more like "screw 'em all if they don't like it but let's make sure everyone gets home safe."

Both of my grandparents have been gone for over twenty years now but I've thought about them a lot while writing this book. I wonder what they would say if they were around to read it today. Part of me worries my grandmother would have been hurt by such a public and light-hearted recounting of my journey away from Catholicism, something that was so special to her.

But I think she'd mostly be proud; she had a pretty good handle on the whole unconditional love thing. I like to picture her giving me her famously gentle *I-love-you-but-let's-think-about-our-*

choices-next-time smile while looking down at her eternally single, 40-year-old grandson, covered in tattoos and chain-smoking his way through a bottle of mediocre Scotch while pecking away at a laptop into the wee hours of the night.

"It's really lovely," I imagine her saying. "But you know, it could have done without all the swear words." Fair point, grandma.

From what I understand, both of my grandparents were deeply religious people for most of their lives. But it seemed to get kicked up a notch as they crossed into their seventies, which I imagine is pretty common. Maybe there's something about hearing the clock tick a little louder that makes us all want to double-check our homework before the final bell rings. Whatever the reason, for most of the time I knew them they attended mass every morning. Every. Single. Morning. They were definitely turning in all their homework on time.

Then when I was about ten years old, they went on what would be their final trip. It was a pilgrimage of sorts to Vatican City and all I really remember is the "special gift" my grandmother brought back for me. It was a beautiful dark gray rosary that—by her account—had been personally blessed by the Pope. For all the un-anointed heathens out there, a rosary is basically a necklace of prayer beads with a crucifix attached that you're never, ever, ever supposed to wear. That's like instantly drawing the "Go to Jail" card in Monopoly, except with eternal damnation.

I suspect it's more than likely the shop that sold it to her also sold her on the idea of the Pope himself actually holding that specific rosary in his hands as he said some extra special words. Catholics eat that stuff up—I know I did. And while I can't speak for other religions, we were all about some supernatural accessories during my tenure: magic amulets that grant special protection, water that has miraculous healing power because someone in a robe said some words over it and even medallions that help prevent you from getting lost.

I remember as my grandmother gave me the rosary, there was this extra shimmer in her eyes. It was a look of true faith. She was 100% certain that this very special, holy item would bring blessings to a child she loved dearly. And as far as I'm concerned, that alone was enough to make it magical. The love she poured into it made it my special talisman and I treasured it. If we had the same conversation today, I'm not sure we would agree on where that magic came from—but I think we would both definitely agree it was there.

With the exception of regular visits to my grandparents' apartment, there wasn't much talk about religion in my house growing up. Truth be told, we didn't talk much about anything, let alone tricky subjects like faith. We might have chatted about the logistics of when we were going to mass on Sunday or what I had to wear for my First Communion but that was about as existential as it got. It was a pretty traditional Irish Catholic upbringing in that sense— decades of mastering the fine art of emotional repression and unspoken shame combined with unquestioning faith. Good times were had by all.

My parents were older than most; my dad was in his mid-forties when they decided to adopt their first child and that created a sort of double generation gap where my parents were closer in age to most of my friends' grandparents.

My older sister was first and then in what I'm still convinced was some sort of coupon or discount situation, three years later they picked me up from the baby store. I'm clearly still not 100% certain on how that whole process works but I like to picture a retail shopping experience with all the kids up for adoption on display in a storefront window.

"Yeah, we'll take the chubby one in the corner who keeps drooling on himself," I imagine my mom saying.

Then three years after that came the big surprise—my mom was pregnant. Yeah. The baby of the family was also the only biological child. You can guess how that dynamic played out through the years.

Growing up, we were what I would call "middle-middle class." My dad didn't have a college degree but he entered the work force in the early sixties, a time when starting in a mail room might actually lead to a career that could comfortably support a family one day.

Well . . . if you were white. And a man. And didn't have a last name that sounded too "ethnic." Or speak with any sort of accent.

Having checked all the traditional white privilege boxes, over time my father would come to make a modest, working-class living. Although to this day, I'm still not sure what he did exactly. I think it was an office job that had something to do with housing or construction or both. That's probably a pretty good example of the level of communication that was happening in our house.

Whatever he actually did all day long, it allowed him to build a three-bedroom ranch house in a nice, typically suburban neighborhood in St. Louis, Missouri that he and his wife would end up living in for close to sixty years.

My father wasn't necessarily cheap but he was definitely frugal. His own parents had lived through the Great Depression and I think he inherently felt a sense of duty in not spending money on supposedly "frivolous" things. Growing up, that meant we kept a car until the doors nearly rusted off and never traveled anywhere on vacation that was more than a few hours' drive away by car. Take a peek at St. Louis on a map and behold all the cultural wonders and exotic locales you can visit within a two-hundred-mile radius.

But what he *did* splurge on was his children's education and in so many ways, I'm still incredibly thankful for that. The unspoken condition was that it had to be a Catholic school. That meant I was in "Jesus Academy" from preschool through my senior year of high school. No problem, right? I'm sure I'll manage with little to no lasting psychological issues.

Luckily, it also meant I was unknowingly collecting decades worth of stories that would one day litter the pages of this book. All therapy bills aside, I consider it a fair trade.

⁓

Today, my relationship with Catholicism is a bit complicated. Philosophically, I have serious issues with a huge chunk of what is considered dogma. And it's kind of an "all or nothing" proposal, at least as I learned it growing up in the church. There's no a la carte option. But perhaps even more critically, I have deep ethical issues being part of any organization—whether that's spiritually, politically or professionally—that has outwardly and openly discriminated against women and the LGBTQ+ community, not to mention the decades of rampant pedophilia and subsequent organizationally-supported cover-ups that continue to this day.

But whether I like it or not, my Catholic upbringing is intricately woven into the fibers of my identity—both in its presence and absence. And while I've never been one to pull my punches, I also don't have any interest in attacking someone else's belief system for sport.

Truth be told, I have no idea where I sit on the religious spectrum today. I'm pretty sure I'm not Atheist—I think there's some force or forces other than ourselves at work and part of me needs to believe in a little magic every now and then. I'm not smart enough to be Agnostic but I'll check that box on a survey in a pinch. Just don't ask me to explain what it means at a party. It feels like a lot of philosophy is involved and I'm only any good at philosophy when I'm stoned on my couch talking to my dog.

Then there's this whole "spiritual but not religious" option that seems to keep popping up everywhere, which I'm pretty sure someone in the media has already blamed on Millennials. So SBNR—as I don't think anyone anywhere calls it—feels like the right level of commitment for where I'm at, but holy shit can it be any more pretentious? It just reeks of Whole Foods, colon cleanses and yoga retreats.

I guess the closest I've come to philosophically agreeing with a spirituality is in *Star Wars*. The whole idea of the Force and midi-chlorians and everything in existence being connected on a spiritual level feels like something I can get behind. And I like the duality of the light vs. dark side as elements that perpetually exist within everyone and that there is an ebb and flow to it. Any ideas that start to look at morality more as a gradient and less like a hard line are usually going to get some affirming head nods from me.

And while I'm sure someone much smarter than me could point out that George Lucas based a lot of those ideas on some of the eastern religions, I unfortunately didn't read any of those books. I read comic books. And played video games. And perhaps more importantly, I watched *Star Wars* movies over and over and over again. So that's what stuck.

My exit from Catholicism wasn't really intentional at first and I ended up coming back more than a few times over the years. In the beginning, it was a simple act of emancipation from my alarm clock going off on Sunday mornings. As I entered the corporate workforce after college, every hour of those weekends became precious and I sure as hell wasn't going to get up early and go to church. Oh, and there were hangovers. Lots and lots of hangovers.

But eventually, usually after a handful of years away, I would come back. I think it was mostly because I was missing the sense of community. The church was a huge part of my day-to-day life growing up and there was a certain peace and comfort in the ritual of everything. And typically, it was fine so long as I focused on mindlessly saying the same words for the millionth time. It became almost a meditation of sorts.

But when I returned to the Catholic church again in my early thirties—this time for a girl I was dating—something was different. I was really trying to listen, engage and connect some dots that had been lingering for years. I wanted to genuinely believe but my brain just wasn't buying it. The girl and I split up and I was left holding this half-eaten sandwich of a belief system that I didn't really want to order. But you know . . . if we're stopping, I guess I could eat.

My biggest issues usually popped up during the homily. That's the sort of halftime bit where the priest goes off-script and speaks to the congregation about what they just heard in the gospel. Except priests are human. And give pretty much any human a microphone and a captive audience and eventually the bullshit is gonna start to fly. And traditionally, that's when I would check out.

The last straw came after a particularly brutal couple of years for me emotionally. I had two very close college friends that I considered brothers pass away far too early in life; one in a car accident and one to a cancer diagnosis. They were both incredibly sweet, gentle souls and losing them was crushing for those of us that loved them so dearly. And neither was Christian. If we're keeping score, one was Hindu and the other was Jewish.

Fast forward a few years later to when I was living in Indiana and I'm sitting in a Catholic church listening to Father So-and-So's commentary on the reading. He keeps trying to stick this point that "the only way to heaven is through the acceptance of Jesus Christ as your Lord and Savior."

Next thing I know, my mind is starting to do some morality math and the numbers aren't adding up. This guy is trying to tell me that my friends, who were two of the kindest, most open-hearted people I've ever known, were "not in heaven" because of the team they played for? Which they didn't even pick, by the way. Just like I didn't really pick this team; I inherited my religious beliefs from my parents.

That was the moment organized religion broke for me.

I stood up almost immediately and walked out, dropping an arsenal of military-grade F-bombs under my breath as I left. It all just started to feel like some made-up fuckery meant solely to keep the organization going. Eternal damnation is a pretty intense way to prevent people from window shopping other religions and the constant drive to emphasize there's "only one way" still feels infinitely small-minded to me.

It's like if some of us took Spanish as our second language in high school and some of us took French but then on the final exam, right before graduation, everyone got the Spanish test and was expected to be fluent. You don't pass, you don't graduate. Sorry you were in the wrong class. The correct answer was Spanish.

Muy triste.

Even through all of the fluctuations in my spirituality, I always kept the rosary my grandmother gave me nearby. The beads had become my wishing stones—a sort of hope made tangible—and I found myself still clinging to the magical power within.

But over time, long after my grandmother passed away, a few of the beads started to fall out of the rosary. Then a couple of years later the chain broke. And while I always tried to hang on to it, over decades and several moves, it found its way into the junk drawer, next to my old fraternity pin and a driver's license from two states earlier. Then one day, it was just gone.

I don't remember getting rid of it and I don't know where it went. But I also don't miss it. I don't need it anymore. And that might be about as accurate of a metaphor as I can think of for my relationship with Catholicism today. It was a very special thing that, for a time, I shared with some people that meant the world to me. But those stories just didn't fit me the way they fit them and eventually the beads started falling out, then the chain broke and then I forgot which drawer I put it in. I was growing up.

As my world started to expand and my experiences began to include more and more people that weren't exactly like me, it was harder and harder to believe the way I used to. And while I intentionally left the organization, the choice to turn away from the spirituality was less conscious and more gradual. It just kind of disappeared in the junk drawer.

The good news is that while my individual experiences with the Catholic church may have lacked any sort of divine resolution, they more than made up for it with a colorful cast of characters and all sorts of assorted shenanigans.

I don't claim to know much but what I do know is that if there is a God, he's got one hell of a sense of humor.

TRANSUBSTANTIATION & OTHER FUN WORDS TO PLAY IN SCRABBLE

Looking back, second grade was a pretty monumental year for me. It was the first time I got to pick out my own lunch box and Trapper Keeper during back-to-school shopping (*He-Man* and *Star Wars Return of the Jedi*, respectively). It was also the year I got my first pair of ROOS high-top sneakers.

If you didn't happen to be eight years old in 1985, you may have missed this pop-cultural blip on the radar. The shoes had special zippered pockets where kids could—theoretically—put stuff. That is so long as that "stuff" was the size of a quarter or smaller. So it was really only good for holding a quarter, a few dimes or a pair of nickels. Particularly industrious kiddos might be able to fit two quarters into each pocket but good luck getting those coins back out without some sort of miniature jaws-of-life device.

Unfortunately, I made the same mistake with my first pair

of ROOS that most rookies made by bringing any sort of cash into this sneaker-pocket-storage situation. Hoping to stash that sweet ten-spot your nana gave you for your birthday? Think again, slick. Assuming you were already a master of origami and could somehow fold your precious cargo enough to fit, you'd still be looking at about a 50/50 chance of bill damage when you tried to take it out.

I still remember the sting of that first financial loss based purely on my own stupidity. Sadly, it wouldn't be the last.

Second grade was also a pretty big year for me in the church. My First Confession and First Communion were a few short months apart from one another, though to be fair the ceremonies felt more like an excuse to get presents than any sort of significant spiritual moment.

I was eight and still believed in Santa Claus and the Tooth Fairy. It wasn't too far of a stretch to believe a priest in a booth could make my sins go away and that the bread and wine at mass were being turned into the *literal* flesh and blood of Jesus. My world was still very much full of beautiful magic and if a special bunny could hide eggs filled with candy all over our yard, I was pretty sure I had no reason to doubt the miracle happening at mass every Sunday.

The big difference was that at some point in time, I found out Santa Claus and the rest of the supernatural holiday crew weren't real. That discovery was a bit of a milestone in itself, sort of like my parents finally letting me in on a long-standing prank, albeit after

I had already peeked behind the curtain.

"Don't ruin it for your little sister," my mom would remind me in the hopes I wouldn't spoil the punchline. I remember feeling like a big kid, like I was in on the secret. For the record, I'm still waiting to have that conversation about the sacrament of Communion.

For most of my time in the church, everyone seemed to be maintaining a pretty solid poker face about the specifics of the whole transformation thing during Communion. Just like I had my suspicions about Santa and his elven minions, eventually pockets of doubt surfaced about the whole *literally* turning bread and wine into half-divine flesh and blood.

Even among most (casual) Catholics I know today, this remains a fairly misunderstood and seldom explored concept, especially when presented not as a metaphor but an actual physical / metaphysical transformation. It's such a contentious point that in my early thirties it led to a pretty heated debate with my girlfriend at the time, who was also Catholic.

For whatever it's worth, we both shared the belief that the whole thing was metaphorical but where we disagreed was on the Catholic church's official stance. As I tried hopelessly to explain, the idea is called *Transubstantiation* and it's very much a real part of official dogma.

Beyond being an excellent triple word score in Scrabble, it's the core belief that an actual physical transformation happens every time a priest performs the rite of Communion. As I was taught, it's considered a miracle any time mass happens anywhere. But here's the catch: you can't see, smell or taste the transformation. The substance and essence of the thing has changed but not the outward appearance. So . . . you know, just trust us. It's changed.

One of the most celebrated Catholic philosophers, Thomas Aquinas, put it this way:

"Sight, touch, and taste in thee are each deceived; the ear alone most safely is believed; I believe all the Son of God has spoken, than through his own word there is no truer token."

Moderately clever rhyming aside, at least as I interpret it, he seems to be saying "I believe it's true because Jesus said it's true, despite what my senses tell me." To me, that sounds like a frustrated parent trying to get their toddler to stop asking questions. "Because I said so, that's why."

My girlfriend and I never did resolve our argument, mostly because I couldn't get her to concede the seemingly far-fetched notion that this was a real church teaching. But as I learned it, Transubstantiation is one of the most foundational teachings of Catholicism.

All Jesus-infused cannibalism and vampiric blood drinking aside, First Communion was a big deal in terms of my participation in mass. But once I was old enough to join the adults and older kids during the processional portion of the service, there was a whole new dynamic in play: hyper self-consciousness.

Like a lot of writers, I've always been an avid people watcher. Nothing I can think up in my head will ever be as ridiculous as observing the human animal out in the wilds of society. Despite our best intentions, we are all inches away from absurdity at any moment.

I'm unfortunately far too clumsy in my observations, often pretending I'm hidden behind some sort of one-way glass where me and my fellow researchers can safely take notes. On more occasions than I'd care to admit, I'll accidentally catch direct eye contact with the "subject" and panic like a deer in headlights, as if my secret research project has finally been found out and I need to start shredding the evidence.

To make matters worse, I have a face that likes to prominently display my current emotions on a jumbotron for the whole world to see; my pasty-white Irish hue flushes bright red and I'm found out in an instant.

But now that I was one of the "big kids" who took Communion, my peaceful time at church spent observing the passers-by would be drastically cut in half. I now had to be one of the observed—and I was *not* cool with it. I'm guessing it's like this for most kids but any activity that involved me getting up in front of a group was an instant avalanche of anxiety. Even simply walking up to the front of the classroom to sharpen my pencil left my hands so drenched in sweat I could barely maintain a grip on my trusty #2.

So when it was time to give my report on Liechtenstein to the class, the walk from my desk to the front of the room was the hardest part. It seemed like I could feel everyone's eyes on me and it made my skin crawl. But once I was up there talking, I was OK until I had to walk back to my seat.

Side note: Liechtenstein is apparently the topic you get when the class is doing reports on Europe and you're out sick the day they pick countries. It's also the world's leading manufacturer of false teeth if I recall correctly.

Going up for Communion was all walk and no report. I dreaded it and there was the added pressure of not just other kids in the "audience" but adults and even the Almighty himself watching me. The whole thing felt like a death march; my very own Trail of Tears reenacted every Sunday morning.

I should probably add that even at a young age I had a tendency to lean toward the melodramatic. And by *lean*, I mean swan dive headfirst into emotional hyperbole.

The actual Communion procession—like most things in the church—had a specific order and ritual to it. There can't be anarchy in the aisles, after all. The priest saying mass was always the headliner, so of course he got the main center aisle. But to help with crowd control, there were parishioners who were "specially trained" to hand out the bread and wine, usually positioned to the far left and right of the priest.

And because it's Catholicism, the helpers of course have a special name: *Extraordinary Ministers of Holy Communion* or *EMHC* if you're down with the youth group scene. Personally, I think the whole thing sounds like something straight out of a Marvel comic:

In this issue of Extraordinary Ministers of Holy Communion, we follow the EMHC squad on their latest adventure as they battle the evil Mr. Masturbator and his army of Impure Thoughts. When we last left the team, Captain Celibacy was trapped in a bathroom with a jar of Vaseline and a JC Penney catalog opened to the women's lingerie section. Will temptation get the better of him and forever corrupt his mortal soul? Read on to find out!

Oddly enough, there was a surprising amount of strategy to picking where I sat in church and it played a considerable role in determining my experience when it was time for Communion. It was a delicate balance based mostly on what trade-offs I was willing to make, with the major consideration being how long I was able to tolerate kneeling.

If you've never attended a Catholic mass, there's an awful lot of standing to kneeling to standing to sitting and back again, like one big game of Whack-A-Mole. The idea is that the whole congregation does this in unison, so in most situations it's not like one section of the church is putting in any more kneeler time than another. That is with one exception: there's a small pocket of time during the Communion procession where there's a variable kneeling-to-sitting ratio.

As I remember it from my church days, the bit right before everyone lines up for Communion is a kneeling part. Then the people in the front stand up, form a line and head toward the altar. In the meantime, everyone else sits down until their row is the next to line up. That's the sweet spot and the only breather to be found in this up-down marathon.

I learned to savor it, because once I'd received Communion, I was supposed to go back to my pew and kneel until everyone else was finished with their snack. Depending on how big the church was and how many people were in attendance, it could turn into a bit of an endurance exercise. I'm still convinced it's one of the main reasons so few people sit at the front of the church during a Catholic service; it's hell on the knees during Communion.

Thanks to this little respite, the pews in the back of the church got the longest "sitting down" break. But it came with a cost. Trade-offs, remember? Very generally speaking, the people in the back of the church were the last to arrive, some potentially even—*gasp*—arriving after mass had started. Filthy sinners. Jesus died for your sins. The least you can do is refrain from hitting the snooze button for the fifth time.

Needless to say, there was a fair dose of shame and judgment handed out to anyone who was tardy. That's because the people sitting in the back were also at the end of the line when it was time to walk up to the altar. That meant rows and rows of daggers-shot-from-eyes directed at the late-comers as they made their way back to their seat. Those folks in the front have been kneeling this whole time and frankly they're sick of your shit, Ted.

It was a classic Catholic move and one I had mastered from a young age: I'm going to blame you (silently in my mind, of course) for how long I've had to kneel, instead of . . . oh, I don't know . . . maybe questioning why I can't just sit down during this part. There's a reason the sheep / shepherd metaphors in the Bible resonated so well with me during my tenure.

In the downward spiral of church-attendee shame—just slightly below the denizens of the "last row"—were the *sitters*. These were the folks that, upon returning from Communion, went straight to sitting and skipped the kneeling bit altogether. In general, it was an approved move for the elderly, small children or the noticeably injured or disabled.

I'd like to emphasize *noticeably* because if you were under seventy and not kneeling, I was going to need to see some medical paperwork before detouring any of the passive aggressive, silent judgment I had headed your direction.

Finally, there were the rare, majestic creatures not going up for Communion at all. And I had so many questions for them.

"Who are these untamed savages, these noble rebels?" I would ask myself. "What brought them here? What horrible thing have they done to be banned from Communion? Wait, are they even Catholic? Then why are they here? I *have* to be here and I hate it. Why would anyone volunteer for this? Is this even allowed? Are they a spy for another team?"

It was all far too much for my curiosity to handle. In an instant I'd be thinking up their elaborate backstories.

The older guy three rows back from the choir section not going up for Communion? Former KGB. He's been living in the neighborhood with his wife Ulyana since 1978. They met in a Siberian gulag where he was undercover as a prisoner and Ulyana was working in the kitchens. Every day she would sneak him an extra potato at dinner and every evening before she fell asleep, she would pray to St. Daniel—the patron saint of prisoners—on his behalf.

Then one day, a massive riot broke out. It was madness, chaos everywhere. But through the smoke, our fair maiden saw "Ivan" (which of course isn't his real name because if you knew his real name he would have to kill you). Potato in hand, she rushed toward him. Together they scurried through the smoke and debris, finally making their perilous escape from the prison.

He made a promise to never again be out of her sight, not even for the slightest moment. And to this day, he's kept that promise despite . . . I guess . . . not being Catholic? I don't know. The endings of my daydreams were always interrupted by the priest telling us to "please rise" or something.

Either way, I deduced all of this simply from the fact the elderly gentleman's hat was black and furry and kind of looked like the one Nikolai Volkoff was wearing when he fought Hacksaw

Jim Duggan on *WWF Main Event* the night before.

. . . aaaaaand now we're standing again.

My family always sat in the same section of the church like it was assigned seating. Never one for change, my dad had decades earlier picked out a spot just to the left of the choir, about two-thirds of the way to the back. In what was one of his signature moves, somehow nobody was happy with the decision but nobody was terribly miserable, either. From our regular spot, the kneeling part of Communion was more of a dull, constant pain that I knew would go away eventually and I just had to wait it out. Not unlike growing up in my family.

⟳

It's kind of silly to think of now, but I remember little acts of rebellion flaring up when I was finally old enough to drive myself to church. I'd usually try to go solo and reveled in the pseudo-independence of it all.

"Forget this 8:00 a.m. malarkey—I'm sleeping in and going to 11:00 a.m. mass. It's a whole other crowd at those shows. And I'm going to sit wherever I damn well please!"

As advertised, it was a *slightly* different experience. The choir sounded a little tinnier from the other side of the church. The "peace be with you" part involved a whole different set of hands to shake. And if I was one of the ne'er-do-wells in the back, I could sneak into the school for a quick bathroom break.

In truth, all I'd really do was meander the halls for a few minutes as sort of a self-imposed church recess. In most other situations, I couldn't have cared less about the fourth-graders' science fair posters hanging in the school lobby. But during my little mid-mass getaway? I was diligently reading through each thesis like I was trying to find the cure for cancer.

But the real prize of going to mass by myself was plotting and executing my secret-agent-in-training escape plan at the end. I'd picked up a few of Ivan's old KGB tricks. The whole Communion portion of mass typically takes place about forty-five minutes into the hour-long service and is kind of like the last song the headlining band plays in their set; we all know there's going to be an encore but enthusiastically go along with the ruse anyway.

"What's this special treat? The band is coming back on stage because we've given them such a rousing ovation? We seem to have applauded our way into bonus content. What an original and not-at-all expected outcome!"

At concerts, this is when I head for the exit; I'm usually done "people-ing" at this point and would rather sneak out early to beat the traffic. The last few songs make a fine soundtrack for my walk to the car as I grin smugly to myself knowing I won't be one of those suckers stuck in the parking lot for an hour trying to get out.

That curmudgeonly old man concert-going approach has its origins directly rooted in my earliest solo church experiences.

Once the actual Communion host hit my lips, it was like the band playing their most popular single. I got what I came for and the rest of the service was mostly more ritualistic choreography with an announcement or two thrown in for good measure. I really didn't need an update on last weekend's fish fry or the choir's next fund-raiser.

So after Communion, instead of heading back to my seat, I'd nonchalantly keep walking past my pew until I was safely in the parking lot. And then POOF! Another successful execution of *Operation: Holy Ghosted.*

HOLY WATER & HULKAMANIA

Growing up in St. Louis meant I was lucky enough to be in one of the few markets at the time that televised regional professional wrestling, so from a very young age I had the privilege of watching *Wrestling at the Chase*. The show was broadcast live on Saturday nights from the Chase Park Hotel downtown but aired well past my bedtime. That meant I would have to catch the reruns on Sunday mornings once I got back from church with my family.

From the very beginning there was an odd, unexpected connection between coming home from mass and watching grown men violently punch and kick one another. I remember rabidly cheering on Ric "The Nature Boy" Flair as he sauntered into the arena—complete with sequined robe and feather boa— with the taste of Communion host still fresh on my breath. *WOOO!!!*

Eventually I'd come to view both the body slams and Catholicism with the same level of suspicion but as a kid it was all still very real. The priest *really* just turned the bread and wine into Jesus' body and blood and Ted DiBiase *really* just kidnapped "Macho Man" Randy Savage's manager Miss Elizabeth.

Looking back it also strikes me as a bit ironic that despite growing up in an unfortunately intensely homophobic environment, the "manliest" men I knew were all oiled up and rolling around with one another in a ring while wearing little more than their tightie-whities.

By the time the regional shows gave way to the behemoth that would become Vince McMahon's WWE empire, I was already hooked. I had all the toys, the ring, the collectible cards and anything else I could get my hands on.

The monthly television special *Saturday Night Main Event* could have easily been mistaken for a religious holiday in our house. My sisters and I got special permission to stay up late to watch it, all curled up in front of the TV in our pajamas watching George "The Animal" Steele literally eat the stuffing out of the turnbuckles. It was absurd and wonderful and the perfect mix of sports and theater.

I suspect there was a lot more than just scheduling that connected my early experiences of going to church with watching wrestling. They both relied heavily on pageantry: ornately decorated outfits, entrance music, clear distinctions between the good guys and bad guys, lots of choreography, passionate speeches, call-and-answer interactions, all kinds of props and even special holidays (Christmas, Wrestlemania, Easter, Survivor Series).

They also both had helpers. In pro wrestling, often there was a manager or sidekick hanging around just outside the ring, ready to lend a hand at a moment's notice by tossing in a steel chair, shouting through a megaphone, breaking up a pinfall or just generally moving the storyline along. In the Catholic church I attended, those duties fell to the altar servers. And since no one was asking me to help them win the Tag Team Championship any time soon, I enthusiastically joined up with the church's version.

One of the benefits of having received the sacrament of First Communion—in addition to being able to partake in the bread and wine at mass—was that I could sign up to be an altar server. Back then, it was an option only available to boys, the absurdity of which only further illuminates the institutionalized sexism and misogyny that has plagued the church since its earliest days.

Thankfully, that rule was changed in 1994 to include girls in all the fun and games. Now everyone can sign up to be an altar server, but keep in mind the title is a little misleading. *Altar servant* may be more accurate; you're really little more than one of the church's house elves. The good news is that if one of the parishioners gives you a piece of their clothing, you're free forever. Or at least until next Sunday.

At the time, I was genuinely excited about it all; it was another rite of passage that made me feel like a big kid. Better still, it came with special "behind the scenes" access to the church, like I had an exclusive VIP pass. Thankfully, I was one of the lucky ones whose time backstage never involved any inappropriate behavior, unless of course you consider having to wake up for 7:00 a.m. mass on a weekend inappropriate. Which I most certainly did.

The gig also came with an elaborate costume, which was a big plus in my book. I've always loved playing dress-up. Even at a very young age, I had an unusually active imagination. I especially enjoyed rooting around old boxes in our basement for the perfect costume and accessories to help bring my make-believe adventures to life.

It didn't take much: a pair of my mom's old leather go-go boots from the seventies, a musty long-forgotten silk scarf, a hoop clip-on earring and one of my dad's old button-down work shirts transformed me into the most feared pirate to sail the seven seas of suburbia.

I suspect at least part of that imagination came as the factory-default setting in my DNA. In my late thirties I began uncovering more and more of my biological roots and it was a beautifully re-affirming journey to put names and faces to something I've suspected all along: I come from a long line of storytellers and artists. There was something deep in my bones from the very beginning that found solace and a place to call home within the worlds I created in my own mind.

It wasn't all genetic, though. It's an interesting study in nature vs. nurture; while my tendency to daydream and create most likely came preinstalled, I think it was kicked up a notch because I didn't have a lot of playmates growing up. I was the middle child, with one sister three years older and another three years younger. There were no other boys on our street but our neighbors to the right had three girls my big sister's age and older and the neighbors to the left had four girls all younger than my youngest sister. That meant very different options for playtime.

When I tried to hang out with the older girls, they liked to turn me into a living Barbie doll and dress me up in whatever rag-tag, moth-eaten evening gown they could find in the basement, complete with wig and full makeup. While I adored the attention, I hated the fact I had no control over the character development or storyline.

Playing with the younger girls, however, lowered the bar a little too far. They had trouble following my high-concept, lore-driven odyssey of the knight and his squires in search of the long-forgotten caverns of the frost dragon. They just wanted to play *My Little Ponies*. When I tried to work in my Four Horseman of the Apocalypse story arc, more than a few tears were shed.

So more often than not, I was on my own. I learned to enjoy my own company, something that as an adult has come to be both a blessing and a curse.

From the beginning, wearing costumes on the outside changed how I felt on the inside. I learned to project myself as an imagined persona I invented in my head; my magical outfits let me become someone other than me, if only for a little while. Looking back as an adult—and with the help of consistent professional therapy—I can see more clearly that my love of dressing up and pretending to be someone else was one of the ways I coped with issues of self-identity and my adoption.

I'm not sure when we stop calling things costumes and start referring to them as uniforms but it seems to happen pretty early on. I had a uniform for school and when I put that on, it meant I was in student mode. I had a uniform for sports and when I wore that one, I was in competitive mode. And when I put on my altar server uniform, I was in piety mode. I was a humble servant of our Lord and Savior Jesus Christ. That was a heavy uniform to wear.

I took my job as an altar server very seriously. Probably a little too seriously, considering I was susceptible to regular fainting spells. In case you're wondering, having a server drop like a sack of potatoes mid-mass can be a little distracting, especially considering I would have to be helped up and hurried off to the sacristy (the backstage area).

There were several theories among my family on why I kept falling over as if a hypnotist had said SLEEP. It was probably *not* that I was overcome by the Holy Spirit, despite my grandmother's not-so-subtly-hidden hopes. I think she was secretly praying one of her grandkids would be a future saint. Then she got to know us and those hopes quickly evaporated.

My father's theory was that my fainting was the same thing he had seen in his brief stint in the military. He would explain how in boot camp, when they made everyone line up in formation, there were usually a few guys who would faint because they "locked their knees," whatever that was supposed to mean.

I wasn't so sure my knees had a locking feature. It seemed like bending was pretty much the main function but admittedly I hadn't read the manual cover-to-cover, so maybe I missed something.

Then there was my mother's hypothesis, which assumed I was doing it to get attention. In her mind I had somehow gained the ability to make myself faint at will and was using it to get out of church. She always had an elaborate explanation for my behavior that greatly overestimated my ability to control involuntary bodily functions.

I have reason to believe my mother viewed many of my uncontrollable physical reactions as a child like vomiting, diarrhea or even a runny nose as intentional acts on my part meant solely to annoy her.

I remember recklessly playing with a box-cutter I found in the basement when I was around ten or so and accidentally slicing my thumb open. I was most likely wounded while performing a brilliant parry and riposte during my duel with the ogre that lived in the utility closet, but I kept those details to myself.

I made my way up the stairs from the basement to the kitchen, leaving a trail of blood droplets in my wake. As I opened the door and took a few steps into the kitchen, my mom—who was on her hands and knees scrubbing the linoleum tile floor—let out a banshee-like squawk about how I was getting blood all over the kitchen floor she had just mopped.

Not sure what to do, I went back downstairs, out the back door and over to a neighbor's house. The nice older couple who lived there promptly bandaged me up and sent me on my way. I may have even gotten some ice cream out of the deal.

I'm sure my mom was more than a little embarrassed I had gone next door for medical attention, and she did show genuine concern when she realized what happened. That was just kind of her way when I was growing up. It wasn't that she was intentionally cruel or insensitive—she simply had really clumsy initial instincts and her emotional intelligence left a lot to be desired. When combined with my heightened emotional sensitivity—especially as a child—it led to some consistently difficult interactions for both of us.

That said, I would think the most common reaction to any

child bleeding in your kitchen would be concern for their well-being with less of an emphasis on what the implications were for your to-do list for the day.

We never landed on an accurate diagnosis for what brought on my fainting spells at church and it never happened in other situations. I've fallen off my fair share of barstools, but that cause-and-effect has never been much of a mystery.

Altar servers in my church spent most of their time rotating between simple tasks like holding up an ornate book called the missal in front of the priest so he could do all the appropriate hand gestures, carrying a cross during the entrance procession, lighting candles, bringing the hotel-mini-fridge-sized bottles of water and wine to the priest right before Communion and ringing a bell on cue as the "miracle" of Transubstantiation happened.

But mostly it was a lot of standing around; we were little more than decoration. That left a lot of moments where it felt like the people in the pews were watching me and—when there wasn't any sort of task to do that would otherwise occupy my anxious mind—I suppose fainting was my brain's way of checking out of the situation.

Although I have to say I really wish the fainting spells had been intentional. That would be a handy trick to have up my sleeve as an adult. It's an easy out for most situations with little to no negative repercussions, provided you have a safe landing.

Stuck in another two-hour meeting at work, listening to Cheryl read word-for-word from her PowerPoint presentation on the cost analysis of switching from 2" wingnuts to 2.25" wingnuts? Aaaaaaaand sleep.

Blind date takes a horrible turn when she starts to read from her *Fifty Shades of Ruth Bader Ginsberg* fan fiction? Buh-bye.

It seems like it would be a clean, if not super clumsy, escape plan. You can't be mad at someone who just fainted. They've experienced a medical emergency, for crying out loud. You give them a glass of water, maybe a damp washcloth and nod solemnly as they explain how this "never usually happens to them" and they "probably shouldn't have skipped lunch." Everyone sympathizes and someone helps them to their car while offering one last sincere "we're just happy to see you're feeling better." It's the perfect guilt-free getaway.

LET'S MAKE A DEAL

There was a brief moment in time at the end of the eighties where I considered myself a skateboarder. It's closer to the truth to say I owned a skateboard I used occasionally to get from point A to point B. The only trick I could do with any consistency involved losing my balance at high speeds and bailing into the nearby grass with limbs akimbo, flailing wildly.

Of course, I wasn't really into skateboarding to actually skateboard. As a form of transportation, riding my bike was far more efficient with less chance of me getting thrown like I was trying to tame a bucking bronco. What interested me most about skating was the culture: the cool clothes, the artwork on the decks and the excuse to use words like "rad" and "killer."

I was way more into putting on the uniform and playing the part than clumsily attempting to jump some kid's homemade "ramp" that was usually little more than a few pieces of warped, splintered plywood hastily pieced together using rusty nails.

My skateboarding uniform always started with the shoes. I was probably in fifth grade when I got my first pair of turquoise high-top Chucks, brimming with pride as I laced up the canvas sneakers for the first time. Considering the legendary shoes were little more than a swath of cloth sewn into a rubber soul, there wasn't much in the way of ankle or foot support.

Fortunately, that wouldn't be too much of a problem. Most of my "skate sessions" consisted of little more than me pushing off to the top of one of the small hills in my suburban neighborhood then letting gravity take care of the ride down. It wasn't exactly an intense athletic activity requiring special footwear.

The perfect pair of shorts were almost as important as the shoes. Culturally, at least in the Midwest while I was growing up, we were just starting to make our way out of the awkward phase where men's shorts looked like something you'd see on a waitress at Hooters, stopping around the mid-thigh area.

Thankfully, with the rise in popularity of sports like skateboarding and surfing, eventually the length of our collective shorts started the long-awaited journey toward the knees.

I gravitated toward this new style almost immediately, considering it a lifesaver. I was really insecure about my thighs when I was a kid, thinking they were far too plump, ashamed that they jiggled when I walked. I imagined the kids in my gym class referring to me as "thunder thighs" behind my back. It was all in my head, of course. No such name-calling ever happened. Everyone was far too wrapped up in their own insecurities to notice mine.

These new "jam shorts" were longer, baggier and usually featured obnoxiously bright neon colors mixed in with images of fruit or some tropical flowers, abstract stripes, dots or random geometric shapes. The louder, the better. It's pretty cringeworthy to look back on now but at the time, I was all about my jams. They instantly became a staple of my wardrobe anytime I could get out of my stuffy, starched Catholic school uniform.

One fateful summer day—decked out from head-to-toe in my best gear—I decided to hop on my skateboard and explore a few distant neighborhoods a mile or so away from my house. With the whole day to spare and the freedom of being unsupervised as long as I was "playing outside," it was all blue sky and open sidewalk as far as the eye could see. I was a pioneer, a brave explorer in a hot pink tank top.

After an hour or so of skating around and soaking in the newly-discovered scenery, I started to make my way back home. About halfway through my return journey, I started to feel a familiar gurgle in my stomach. My digestive system was giving me a few warning shots that there was about to be a situation. It's a gamble we've all experienced at one point or another: look for a bathroom immediately or push your luck and try to make it to the sanctuary of your home commode.

Phase one was denial.

I simply pretended my stomach was acting up because I was hungry, despite the fact I knew full well these were not at all hunger pangs. A quick survey of my surroundings revealed nothing other than rows and rows of cookie-cutter houses, none of them belonging to anyone I knew. There was no way I was going to walk up to a stranger's house and politely ask if I could unleash the storm brewing in my gut into their toilet bowl.

To make matters more desperate, there were no signs of retail stores, gas stations or fast food restaurants anywhere on the horizon—it was all residential for what seemed like miles. Having limited options, I ignored the digestive rumblings as best I could.

Phase two was panic.

I was starting to cramp up and the simple act of riding my skateboard was getting difficult. I had transitioned to walking but in a sort of zombie-like shuffle that was both slow and sporadic. I may have been trying to ignore the call of nature, but nature had no intention of staying silent.

The call got louder and louder with every step. Quickly realizing what was happening, I knew I was in serious trouble. This was an emergency that needed to be dealt with immediately but at my current pace I was at least thirty minutes from home.

In an attempt to defuse the situation, I placed a risky bet I could harness the power of the wind—and my sphincter—by letting out little spurts of gas until the feelings passed. The problem was this greatly overestimated my ability to control my own bodily functions.

The first release was a short, controlled burst of air that, other than the unusual amount of caution and care involved, pretty much went as expected. But it did little to calm the waves in my stomach. Ever-persistent, I repeated the technique, this time with a very different result. Like a sleepy turtle waking up from a nap by slowly poking his head out of his shell, I had unexpected company. This was happening and there was going to be very little I could do to stop it.

I quickly scurried in between two random houses, hid myself away from the road and attempted to take care of my business. Before my knees could even bend into a squat, a dog started barking aggressively from behind one of the wooden fences. The same digestive system that was in such a hurry to do what needed to be done suddenly had stage freight.

Between the dog barking and the distinct lack of pooping on my part, I realized it wasn't going to happen. I pulled up my bright blue jams with neon orange stripes and continued painfully on my way.

Up to this point in my life, the power of prayer was something I fully believed in. Every night before bed, I'd be sure to include some original commentary along with my *Hail Marys* and *Our Fathers*. Whether it was an extra-special request, gratitude for something that happened or simply recounting the highlights of my day, in my head it was a conversation. I had a personal relationship with God and felt like we had established a certain rapport up to this point.

So calling in a favor from the Big Guy in my time of need didn't feel particularly selfish. Not pooping my pants seemed like a win-win for everyone.

It was the earliest iteration of a game I liked to play with God called *Let's Make a Deal*. The Almighty was a loan shark and I was a desperate gambler who was positive he could make his money back with one big bet; I was ready to negotiate very favorable terms in exchange for immediate assistance.

I quickly offered up a verbal contract that stated if I made it home stain-free, I would throw away all of the Victoria's Secret mailers that I had intercepted and was hording under my bed. The trouble with these negotiations with God was that the dialogue was pretty one-sided, so there wasn't exactly a lot of opportunity for feedback, negotiation or confirmation. I had to just assume we had a deal.

This would be the first of many such contracts with the divine that I would enter into over the years. As an adult, these agreements would usually happen when my head was resting on a toilet bowl after far too many pints. I've made many slurred, barely-conscious proclamations to God that "this . . . this is the last time, ever. I swearrrrrrrrrrrr." I usually start to drift off toward the end of my newly-formed covenant but seeing as how I've yet to choke on my own vomit in my sleep, I'd say the terms were agreed to by all parties, despite the fact I had no intention of keeping my end of the bargain once I sobered up.

Unfortunately, me and the Big Guy didn't seem to have a deal on this particular occasion. Cramped up and now breaking into a cold sweat, all it took was the slightest lapse in concentration and the party started. Before I could do anything about it, I was in the midst of the healthiest and most solid movement I think I've ever experienced. Within seconds it felt like someone had dumped a bag of charcoal briquettes into the back of my jams.

It had finally happened, and the release was just as much mental as it was physical. While I was deeply disappointed God had reneged on our deal, at least there was no more suspense. I was mortified but the worst was over.

Phase three was acceptance.

I had shit my pants and was at least thirty minutes from home with nothing but my skateboard, which was now being held awkwardly behind my back in an attempt to cover up the clearly visible lump in my shorts. I suppose I could have emptied my unwelcomed cargo somewhere along the way, but I wasn't exactly thinking clearly in the moment. I was too busy trying to not die of humiliation and embarrassment.

I was also almost immediately hit with a wave of moral and ethical disappointment. How could I believe in a God who didn't intervene to prevent things like kids with cancer, senseless violence and spontaneous jam shitting? My faith had clearly been shaken.

Eventually, I made it home with little to no dignity left. I stealthily snuck into the house through the basement and dropped the kids off at the pool, as they say. But now I had another situation to deal with: my once white underpants had turned a distinct shade of brown.

Quickly realizing they were beyond repair, my mind shifted to disposal. I stashed the stained britches at the bottom of a trashcan by the bar in our basement and hoped to erase my fecal misadventures from my mind. It was usually my dad who emptied that bin and in truth, I gave very little thought to the smell. I had been brewing in my own mess for a while and I guess I got used to the foul odor, not giving a thought to masking it. I clearly miscalculated how distinct the smell of human feces is, especially when encountered in an indoor setting that's not a bathroom.

Less than twenty-four hours later, there was a knock on my bedroom door. It was my dad, wearing a pair of gardening gloves, holding the evidence of the previous day's disaster.

"Want to tell me what this is all about?" he prodded.

Of course I didn't. I was trying to purge the experience from my memory.

"I was playing out in the woods behind Jake's house and we slide down a hill that was all muddy," I lied.

It was a completely impractical excuse. Had I been wearing nothing but my underwear while sliding down this hill with my buddy? Because my t-shirt seemed to be perfectly clean. The smell gave it away and any other explanation was a waste of creativity.

"I won't tell your mom. Just . . . if this happens again, tell me instead of throwing your clothes away," my dad explained, nearly as mortified as I was.

My father's reaction was empathetic embarrassment and we were both eager to put the incident behind us. He knew if my mom found out, it would be a whole "thing" and neither of us wanted that.

Maybe it was all part of God's ultimate plan. Maybe the whole experience was so that one day I could share one of the most embarrassing moments of my life with complete strangers. Maybe God has better things to do than regulate the bowel movements of some random kid skateboarding through suburbia.

If I ever find myself in a situation like that again, I'm making a deal with the devil instead. At least then the terms will be clear.

SORRY, NOT SORRY

When you attend Catholic schools for as long as I did and you start asking enough questions, there's a point where you can tell the priests, nuns and teachers start to wing it. I can't blame anyone for that; a solid majority of them were good people just trying to do what they believed was right. They're human. And it's right before lunch. And their car's in the shop. And Josh just threw up in the hall.

So when my curiosity and logic would start to catch up with what I was learning and I started peppering them with questions, it didn't always go so well. The whole *what happens to good people when they die if they're not Christian* conundrum in particular seemed to bring the most consistent frustration. I'd usually get a dead-end response that referred me back to the "unknowable mystery of God" or the garden-variety "all part of His plan so just have faith."

Translation: "Please shut up, kid. You're going to be late for gym class."

But I needed something tangible because the whole "just have faith" thing wasn't adding up. To me, it felt like a cop-out. It was the gaudy red baseball cap of spirituality with "Make Eternity Great Again" written all over it.

In truth, my journey through Catholicism wasn't nearly as rebellious—or intellectually virtuous—as I like to remember. I wasn't on some spiritual quest for answers and enlightenment; I really just had some clarifying questions around the homework assignments. I genuinely wanted to be "good," whatever I thought that was at the time, but even from early on that felt like a moving target. Thankfully, there was a way to hit the reset button in case I screwed up: Confession.

The premise of the sacrament of Confession as I learned it is that it's a sort of oil change for your soul. Every few hundred sins or so you pop in for some routine maintenance by telling the priest that you're really sorry, he absolves you of those sins, you say a few *Our Fathers* and a handful of *Hail Marys* and you're on your way.

In most Catholic churches there's the option of either face-to-face or "anonymous" confession through a screen. Well, anonymous unless you were the stinky kid, the first to have their voice drop or the one with the wheezy asthma. Sorry, Becky. We all know it's you.

And if you're wondering who chooses the face-to-face option, that one's easy: psychopaths. That's who goes into this situation face-to-face. Want an early screening method for potential serial killers? Post up a child protective services agent just outside the "face-to-face" door of a confessional. You see a kid reach for it, you get them into custody immediately. If they're not already torturing small animals, they will be soon.

As the years went on, I started to develop a tried-and-true strategy for my time "in the booth." For starters, being the not-small-animal-torturing kiddo that I was, I always chose the anonymous option. For those who haven't had the pleasure, the whole routine starts with a sort of password prayer. There was already a distinct Prohibition-era speakeasy vibe to the whole thing, but this took it to the next level.

You're supposed to say something like "Bless me Father, for I have sinned. It's been ____ (amount of time) since my last confession." So right from square one, there's this sharp sense of guilt and shame, which is a combo Catholicism may hold the patent for, if not full copyright in perpetuity. And I was never quite sure how specific to get during this part—are we talking days, weeks, months—so I would usually offer up a humble "It's been a while, I can't remember exactly" and just pile that up with the other sins I already felt shitty about.

Looking back, something always felt a little off about that part. I get that I needed to say what I did and apologize. That's a hard learned but incredibly valuable lesson for any personal relationship, whether it be with my partner or the creator of the universe. So saying I was sorry was usually very cathartic.

But making me say how long it's been since the last time I apologized? Isn't God omniscient? I would think he at least has some sort of spreadsheet where he's keeping track of all this. Making me say it out loud feels like a dick move, like the priest is this sort of guilt and shame traffic cop who has to meet a monthly quota.

After acknowledging my attendance record, it was time to dig into the real dirt. But not without a bit of tactics. First off, I'd never go all in and lead with the worst stuff. That's an amateur move. Instead I'd start by offering up a few sacrificial lambs to get things going.

"I teased my sisters and called them names."

Safe. Solid. Reliable. Even as a kid I saw my older sister as the coolest thing since sliced bread, so there's no way I was actually teasing her, let alone getting away with it. Attempting any kind of shenanigans would result in her and the older neighbor girls relentlessly chasing me around our basement amid chants of "Pooperman," which was about one of the worst things they could call me.

I was—and still am—a huge superhero nerd. I had Spiderman footie pajamas, Batman underoos and even an Incredible Hulk tank top. But my pride and joy was a blue Superman t-shirt with the big S shield on the front that I proudly wore with a matching red cape my mom had made for me. Calling me Pooperman instead of my proper title of Superman, especially when I was in uniform, would trigger an instant temper tantrum.

Back in the booth, I'd continue to throw out a few batting practice sins, mostly keeping things light. Didn't do my chores. Copied Susie's homework. Tried to smoke a cigarette butt I found on the sidewalk—yeah, I know it's gross. I was a constantly curious kid usually left to his own devices. My experiments didn't always go so well.

Overall, I'd keep my confession just specific enough to be real but nothing that would rustle any angel wings. Keep in mind, I still think this whole thing is quite real. As in I get a clean slate if I 'fess up to all my tomfoolery. So I've got some stuff I need to sneak in without Father Bob knowing the illicit details that could get me grounded. Which, ironically, felt like the more pending peril than eternal damnation.

What I was really trying to get to was the fact I shoplifted a bunch of baseball cards and needed that shit expunged from my record. And just like that, I started artfully spouting half-truths.

"I've taken things that don't belong to me."

Accurate? Yes. Truthful? Not so much. But I was learning the loopholes.

Once I had emptied out my sin bin, the priest would give me my penance, which was essentially some sort of action or prayer that I had to do to further show I was sorry.

I gotta say, in all my time in the Catholic church, I don't remember there being all that much variation in punishment from one set of sins to another. Whether I had been in a fist fight at recess or simply stolen a pencil from a classmate, the punishment was almost always ten *Our Fathers* and twenty *Hail Marys* (give or take a handful of repetitions based on severity).

Occasionally a priest would throw in a required apology to a sibling, parent or classmate to spice things up but for the most part it was a fairly predictable punishment that usually just involved repeating some words over and over again.

All told, it was a pretty painless trade-off. And at some point the whole thing became transactional in my mind.

"I really want those baseball cards, but I already spent my allowance," I would think to myself when faced with the inevitable temptation of sin. "OK, so if I steal a few packs that's like thirty or forty *Hail Marys*, right? Done."

I was clearly missing the point.

THE EASTER SPECIAL

For reasons I'll never fully understand, hair was always a big deal in my family growing up. I think my mom secretly had aspirations of being a hairdresser one day and thanks to the fact my dad didn't believe in spending money on things like haircuts, she had a house full of readily available scalps to experiment on.

For as long as I've known her, my mother has had short, tightly permed hair that looks a little bit like a white lady version of Jheri curls. It was a popular look in the eighties for suburban housewives in the Midwest but required significant prep time, and as a result my mother's nightly hair styling ritual took precedence over nearly all other family activities.

Every evening she would sit cross-legged in front of the couch in the living room with a small portable mirror, aerosol can of Aqua Net hairspray and curling iron strategically positioned on the coffee table, looking like a surgeon setting up her instruments before scrubbing in for open-heart surgery. Once her perm was adequately puffed and polished, she would be open for business, ready to accept appointments from other family members.

Being the only boy meant I was the most frequent visitor to her homemade hair salon and quickly became her favorite Chia Pet. She'd try something out and if it didn't quite come out as planned, she'd simply wait for my hair to grow back in a few weeks and try again.

The problem was she wasn't particularly good at any of it. The little bit of acumen she accumulated over the years was more the product of repetition than talent. Ultimately, like so many other mothers of the era, she decided giving me a "bowl" haircut was the simplest, easiest solution.

That atrocious hairstyle stuck with me until the fourth grade, at which point I was somehow able to convince my mom to cut my hair in a more "spiky" style. I wanted something like Bart Simpson's hair, minus the jaundice-yellow hue. To be fair, handing her a picture of a cartoon character and hoping for the same haircut was bound to deliver sub-par results.

As it turned out, my mother's interpretation looked more like a military-style crew cut than one fit for a kid on a skateboard shouting cowabunga. Like so many times before, I would wait for it to grow out and we would try again. But it was better than the bowl—or "butt-cut" as my older sister liked to call it—so we were making progress, if only in baby steps.

Eventually my mother started to see the same spiky haircut pop up on other kids my age, giving her a better idea of what the style was supposed to look like. I owe a great deal to Corey Haim for that one. After a few more tries, she got it close enough that if you squinted and the light was just right, it almost looked like I had gone to a professional barber.

I quickly realized my upgraded haircut came with a new set of responsibilities. I now needed to "do" my hair every morning, much like the evening ritual I'd seen my mother perform for years. The problem was that I didn't know the first thing about styling my hair and there wasn't exactly a professional I could ask for pointers. With the advent of Google and YouTube still a decade or more away, I was on my own. Many mistakes were made.

One of my earliest styling techniques involved filling up the bathroom sink with water until it was nearly spilling over, then dunking my head directly in like I was bobbing for apples. Without even so much as considering a hair dryer or patting down my newly drenched mane with a towel, I'd reach for my trusty can of Rave hairspray, level 4, Mega-Hold. I wouldn't stop spraying until I started to see my own localized hole in the ozone layer.

Within five minutes, that chemical concoction would harden like concrete, creating a sort of spiked hair helmet that could double as a lethal weapon. Not only was this stone-like hairstyle incredibly uncomfortable, but as the day wore on if I accidentally ran my hands through my hair it would create flakes of dandruff-like hairspray dust that would leave a trail wherever I went like a snake shedding its skin. Combined with my early-onset acne—that I'm sure was further agitated by all the product soaking into my skull—it was quite the sight.

Thankfully, there was an emerging expert living in our house in the form of my older sister. Three years my senior, she had been around the hairstyling block quite a few times before I'd even spritzed my first follicle. Locally famous for the sheer heights she could achieve when styling her bangs, her skills with a can of hairspray and a teasing comb were legendary.

While her classmates were in awe, the fashion-forward style seemed to be a magnet for the wrath and fury of the nuns in our little Catholic school. On more than one occasion, she was sent to the principal's office to remove the "pancake batter" from her face, the term bitter, withered-up sixty-year-old virgins used to describe makeup.

~

My two sisters shared a room for nearly eight years despite the six-year age gap between them. We lived in a small three-bedroom ranch house and—being the only kid in the family that stood as he peed (usually)—I won the solo suite. But as my older sister started to enter adolescence, her roommate situation was becoming a form of slow torture.

I give her a ton of credit for lasting as long as she did. If the situation was reversed, I'm quite sure I would have had some sort of psychotic break years earlier. Our youngest sister is not the easiest human being to be around.

Having somehow survived the cohabitation without any formal aggravated assault charges filed by either sibling, my older sister finally convinced our dad to build her a bedroom in our partially-finished basement. While my father was moderately handy, this would undoubtedly be testing his mettle. After enlisting the help of two neighbors, working through three months of weekends and countless cases of Busch beer, the bedroom was complete.

There were no windows, only one or two electrical outlets and a year-round chill to the stagnate, musty air. But it was hers and hers alone and came with the added benefit that the basement bathroom—which was little more than a sink and a commode—was now also part of her private domain. The tiny bathroom that was barely bigger than a closet would become her primping palace, with the sink, walls and mirror constantly covered in a thick residue of hairspray and foundation powder.

My older sister has always been an instinctively nurturing human being. She was the kind of kid you could tell from the very beginning was going to be a great parent one day. She has a naturally kind heart, is slow to anger and was easily the best-behaved child in the family, a fact reinforced by our mom's decision to dress her as an angel for three consecutive Halloweens.

For the record, I had a five-year run in a homemade devil costume.

Not surprisingly, when my sister realized how much I was struggling with styling my hair, she stepped in to graciously lend her expertise. There was also the issue that since we went to the same school, having me walk around looking like I had just stuck my finger in a light socket was going to be a PR problem for her.

Every morning before school for the better part of a year, I would excitedly scamper down the stairs to my sister's private hair and makeup studio for my exclusive appointment. Using whatever photos of teen heartthrobs she had cut out of that month's *Tiger Beat* magazine as inspiration, she would do her best with what she had to work with.

I absolutely cherished the attention; it was an oasis of tenderness amid the dry, emotionally lifeless desert that was the family I grew up in. In our house, being openly kind and loving to another family member was about the most hardcore rebellious, alternative thing you could do. And by those standards, my older sister was punk rock as fuck.

You would think with all the benevolence my sister showed me that I would have returned the sentiment in kind. But I was the one in the devil costume, remember? While I was never intentionally hurtful or mean toward her, I would take advantage of her generosity in some pretty underhanded ways.

Case in point: Shortly after moving into the basement, my sister quickly realized she would now have more than the usual number of unwanted visitors in the form of various bugs, ants and spiders. We quickly made a deal that she would pay me to be her on-call exterminator. If I remember correctly, the going rate was a nickel for ants, a dime for moths and a quarter for spiders.

For the first few months, business was booming. I'd have some sort of insect to squish every few days and my piggy bank was getting fed regularly. But then business dried up, likely due to a change in the weather. Which was bad for my budget. I had been getting enough side work for at least one extra pack of baseball cards a week. In order to keep the cash flowing in, I started hunting for various bugs in the backyard then sneaking them into my sister's room.

I know— I'm the worst.

Eventually I was found out and if I recall correctly some sort of repayment plan was set up. Yet despite all that, she was quick to forgive and even quicker to call my name when her spider friends came around again.

~

For all my visits to my mom's homemade hair salon, there is one haircut in particular that I've requested be redacted from the records entirely, hoping to burn all photos and avoid any future mention of the incident. For an entire school year, my hair was cut in a style I shamefully refer to as "the Missouri Compromise."

Yes, I had a mullet.

Business in front, party in back, embarrassment everywhere. As if the short-long combo wasn't bad enough on its own, there was my mom's brilliant idea to perm the back to help "make it pop."

It was a disastrous combo somehow made even worse by the addition of what was called a "rat tail"—a few strands at the bottom of my white-trash waterfall left intentionally longer than the others, hence resembling the curly tail of a rodent. My mother—who was clearly preparing me for a career as a cashier at Walmart or a long-haul truck driver—not only let me walk around with this travesty but intentionally and actively participated in its creation.

Thankfully there is only one known picture from that time period and it haunts my nightmares to this day. It was Christmas morning and the photo features ten-year-old me posing on a floral-patterned, olive-green sofa proudly wearing a black Def Leppard *Hysteria* t-shirt and baggy acid-washed jeans, showing off my shiny new black electric guitar with built-in amplifier that my parents bought from Kmart, hot pink guitar strap slung over my shoulder.

But the real highlight of the photo is the trailer trash hairstyle I'm wearing that showcased a heavily hair sprayed spiked front, matted-down middle that somehow looked like it was borrowed from another head of hair and a cascade of unnatural curls in the back. It was all utterly unforgivable.

Given my mother's history of experimentation with my hair, it seemed like a natural evolution that I would take matters into my own hands at some point. Knowing she would not agree with my assessment, I kept her in the dark as I snuck a pair of electric hair clippers into my sister's bathroom one fateful morning. It was the week before Easter during my eighth-grade year, so I was probably fourteen at the time and primed to make some really rash decisions.

Having never used a pair of clippers before, I was blissfully unaware that the different guards for the blades resulted in different lengths. I matter-of-factly went about my business with no guard at all. As you might expect, nearly as soon as the humming blades touched my scalp, I realized the mistake I made and was instantly flooded with regret.

Now that I had a significant chunk of hair missing from the right side of my head, just above the ear, there was little choice but to keep going. I had fallen in a hole and was going to dig my way out of it instead of calling for help.

It was partially because I knew the verbal ass-whipping that was headed my way and I wanted to delay the inevitable for as long as I could. With all the coordination and grace of a drunken sailor on shore leave, I continued the butchery until all the hair on the sides and back of my head was nothing but a distant memory.

Considering there was no fade and just an abrupt stop, my masterpiece left me looking like Moe from the Three Stooges, an ironic and unsettling throwback to the "bowl" haircuts I hated so much as a child. I had come full circle in a disastrous yet self-inflicted parade of poor choices.

My options were pretty limited at this point. I could run away, taking my binders of baseball cards and collection of CDs in the hopes of bartering for food and shelter while living on the streets until my hair grew back but I didn't really want to part with the music or the cards. I could wear a bandanna and pretend to be a chemo patient until I had a full head of hair, but that felt far too disingenuous. The only real option was to admit to my crimes and hope for a swift and just punishment.

After seeing my mangled mop, my father somewhat nonchalantly laughed it off. In his opinion, my punishment was simply having to walk around with that atrocious haircut until it grew out. No hats, no bandannas, no hoodies. I had to own it. That seemed fair enough.

Unfortunately, he and my mother were not on the same page and little could have prepared me for her reaction when she saw what I'd done. She was furious and ashamed and beside herself all at once. It was anger mixed with embarrassment in equal measure, but not embarrassment *for* me like when you watch a really bad karaoke performance or elementary school musical. It was embarrassment that I was her son.

It was almost as if I had taken the clippers to her own hair while she was sleeping and shaved her bald for the fun of it. Her reaction didn't seem to match what happened and to this day I still have no idea what triggered her intensity.

Her biggest concern was what to do about the upcoming Easter Sunday mass. As she explained to me in very clear and direct terms, she was ashamed to be seen in public with me. But there was no way I was getting out of going to church. She knew that would be more reward than punishment.

Instead, my punishment was to go to church with the family as planned except I wasn't allowed to sit with them. I had to stand in the back by myself.

I can see now as an adult how deeply the experience damaged my relationship with my mother. Excluding and ostracizing an adopted child who was old enough to intellectually and emotionally understand what was happening was shameful enough but doing it publicly and in a religious setting was somehow even worse. Unfortunately, that was just sort of her way and my father was just as guilty for going along with it.

Eventually my hair grew back and we all returned to our normal routines. A few months later, I got my first part-time job and finally had a little spending money of my own. My first big purchase? A visit to a professional barbershop.

THE MITZIS THREE

My parents have owned three dogs since they've been married, each one bearing witness to a significant chapter in their lives. The first of these canine companions was brought home years before the arrival of any children, a moment in time still labeled CLASSIFIED all these years later, like a hastily covered up UFO sighting. I didn't have the proper security clearance to ask too many questions as a kid and the only evidence of this animal ever having existed has long-since been hidden away in forgotten photo albums buried in the basement.

If the rumors are true, somewhere in those dust-covered albums are top-secret black-and-white photos of a top-secret black-and-white rat terrier that roamed the house freely around 10 BC (Before Children). If you chase the paper trail even deeper, supposedly there was also a pet parrot and a pair of bunnies, which still blows my mind and feels more like fiction than historical fact.

My parents were legendarily mundane human beings and my mother was borderline fanatical about the cleanliness of her home. This mysterious past life as the owners of some sort of emerging menagerie seems so out of character that I wouldn't be surprised to discover they had both been abducted by aliens and lobotomized prior to having kids.

It was the late sixties and in a move I can only hope was some sort of culturally relevant inside joke at the time, they named their first dog Mitzi.

When asked years later if they choose the moniker as an ode to Mitzi Gaynor—possibly the only famous person to ever bear the name—my parents would offer a simple "No, she wasn't named for the actress. We just liked the name." Their over-simplified reasoning only further emphasized the bullet I dodged when they named me. I have my suspicions I was a few stiff cocktails away from being a Humphrey, Marlon or Laurence. Just because they liked the name, of course.

Naming choices aside, Mitzi the canine was apparently quite aggressive. Maybe it was restlessness due to the distinct lack of rats available to chase or simple rebellion against the name she was given but if the stories are to be believed, Mitzi behaved like she was part demon.

The urban legend around our house growing up was that the twelve-pound hellhound—in a fit of rage—took a bite out of my uncle's nose, leaving part of his nostril dangling in the wind. That same uncle made a point of showing me the scar nearly every Thanksgiving as if it were our own little morbid tradition as he passed the mashed potatoes. I'd seen the handiwork of Satan's lapdog firsthand.

Not surprisingly, it wasn't long after my dad paid the emergency room bill for the damages his dog had inflicted that Mitzi mysteriously disappeared, her existence removed from all official documents.

When I was in fourth grade, my mom came across a photo in the newspaper of a dog she swore looked exactly like the Mitzi from years earlier. Same breed, same coloring, same size.

Since all three of us kids were old enough to pretend to take care of the animal, we planned a visit to our local Humane Society that same day. Within a few short hours we were welcoming home the newest member of our family.

This new rat terrier was a near-perfect clone of my parents' original, so when discussions began about what to call her, you can probably guess which name was the leading candidate. With little debate, we enthusiastically welcomed another Mitzi into our clan.

Considering how young we were and that it was a seemingly democratic vote, I suppose it could have been worse. My older sister's kids—who are about the same age now as we were when we got our dog—were also given a choice in naming the pair of barnyard kittens they recently adopted. Those same cats now respond to *Mr. Pickaxe* and *Creeper*, respectively—her kids play a lot of Minecraft.

Mitzi Two was a sweet, even-tempered and unusually tolerant little pup, gracefully enduring the roughhousing she received at the hands of three overly exuberant kids. But as it is with most dogs in a multi-member family, there's usually one of their humans they recognize early on as the commander-in-chief. For Mitzi Two, that person was unequivocally my mother. That was the first lap our Mitzi looked for and within weeks she took up a permanent residence next to my mom at the foot of her bed.

At some point during that first year, Mitzi Two started to suffer from violent seizures. Our normally peaceful, affectionate companion would begin to shake uncontrollably while foaming at the mouth, suddenly becoming incredibly aggressive, completely unaware of her surroundings.

Her sudden shift in behavior was undoubtedly an involuntary reaction to the fear and confusion brought on by the seizures, but as a kid it was terrifying to watch. She would show her teeth while making unnatural sounds like she was possessed by some evil entity. It was as if by giving her the same name as the Mitzi before her, we had unknowingly cursed her, giving the tormented spirit of Mitzi One the opportunity to exact her revenge from the grave.

Thankfully, exorcising the demon of "The One Who Came Before" was made considerably easier with the help of prescribed medication taken on a daily basis. Once the fits and seizures were under control, Mitzi Two lived a happy, comfortable life as a trusted sidekick, quickly learning which of us kids was more likely to take her on a walk, who would sneak her food from their plate and who gave the best belly rubs. Living nearly long enough to get her own driver's license, Mitzi Two eventually passed peacefully of old age while I was away at college.

A few years after I graduated college, I got a call from my mom saying they were thinking of getting another dog. I was thrilled at the news, knowing a four-legged friend would likely be just the distraction she and my dad needed to keep them from murdering one another in their newly-emptied nest.

I've always believed dogs are far better people than humans and injecting some abundant, unconditional love into that house was only going to be a good thing. Then I remembered I had actually met my parents and my enthusiasm began to fade quickly.

"What kind of dog are you thinking about getting?" I asked the question half-knowing the answer.

"Well, we went to the Humane Society and saw the cutest little rat terrier . . ."

She didn't need to finish. The adventurous couple who at one point in time had a dog, a parrot and two rabbits wandering the halls of their home had long since vanished, replaced by two disgruntled roommates who's only shared interests were being uninterested in just about everything.

I played along, not-so-secretly holding out hope that at least they might pick a new name.

"We're going to call her Mitzi," my mom explained before I could muster the courage to ask.

Hearing her matter-of-fact answer left me feeling utterly deflated, like a wrinkling balloon hovering in the corner of a kitchen days after the birthday party has ended. We named the second dog Mitzi because we were silly kids and wanted "our own Mitzi" as if the name were a synonym for dog. But a third Mitzi? It was the trilogy no one needed.

Mitzi Three was an unfortunate byproduct of her environment. She barked more than any dog I've ever met, yapping incessantly at everyone who walked down the street, any critters that entered the yard or any leaves that fell from the trees. And for some unknown reason, my parents seemed to encourage the behavior.

There was an entire decade where every phone call home was accompanied by high-pitched barking in the background for the duration of the conversation, as if Mitzi Three was their youngest child who was throwing a temper tantrum because she wasn't the center of attention in that moment.

Mitzi Three would let you pet her on occasion but she was as finicky as a feline, so if you accidentally scratched behind the wrong ear she was going to let you know by nipping at your fingers. My parents never took her out on walks and playtime was limited to the occasional tug-of-war with a tennis ball stuffed into an old gym sock. The result was a hyper-paranoid, high-strung maniac who was clearly suffering from some significant psychological problems.

I never blamed Mitzi Three for being an asshole. She unfortunately soaked up and reflected my parent's energy, quickly becoming one more voice in their "everything is horrible all the time" choir.

While Mitzi Two was undoubtedly my mom's dog, the tables were turned this time around. My father had since retired and in sort of a baton hand-off of employment, my mother now worked full-time on the factory floor of a company that made commercial cleaning products. That newly inverted dynamic meant Mitzi Three was my dad's shadow, inches from his heels as he shuffled around the house in his slippers.

The two of them would spend most of their days glued to the sofa cushions—each of them had their own separate couch in the basement—while watching hours upon hours of Fox News.

It was almost as if the fear, paranoia and propaganda that was seeping out of the TV on a daily basis changed not only my father's personality but that of his faithful companion as well. They were both terrified of strangers or anything that was different from them and snarled when confronted with things like science and facts.

The third Mitzi died a handful of years ago when my parents were in their mid-seventies. And while I had fears of a fourth iteration, my parent's explanation for why they didn't want another dog hit me harder than I expected. They knew if they got another dog it would likely outlive them and be too difficult to manage if either of them got sick. They were starting to face their own mortality in a way I wasn't ready to hear.

Unfortunately, those words rang true sooner than any of us expected when the early signs of Alzheimer's started to show up in my father, just like his father before him. Not long after, my mother had to move him into a nursing home down the street from the house he had built sixty years earlier. He passed away less than a year later.

While my relationship with my parents over the years has been complicated and unfortunately all too often toxic, no one wants to think about the people that raised them dying. Once I realized there wouldn't be a Mitzi Four, it was a punch in the gut. The Mitzi franchise would forever remain a trilogy and like all things eventually be little more than memories and photos tucked away in dusty albums buried in a basement.

ST. ANTHONY OF CHILI PEPPERS

Like most fourteen-year-olds, during my last year before high school I was only just barely starting to peek my head around the corner into adulthood. Too skittish and unsure of myself to stare for too long, I'd quickly scamper back into childhood the first chance I got.

But whether or not I knew it at the time, I was slowly starting to gain agency in my own life. I was getting my first sense of personal style and developing taste. Even if it was only in subtle ways, I had the power to choose the music I listened to, the clothes I wore and the way I combed my hair.

It was 1991, the same year Nirvana released *Nevermind*. Which is to say I'm pretty sure I was at optimal angst levels to fully ride the wave of "grunge" that followed. All flannel, all the time. Pearl Jam's *Ten*, Red Hot Chili Peppers' *Blood Sugar Sex Magik* and

Soundgarden's *Badmotorfinger* were all released that year as well. Those ground-breaking albums would end up being the soundtrack to my earliest teenage years.

While I was never entirely sure what this "teen spirit" was supposed to smell like, I imagined it to be a bit like my socks after basketball practice if I had then masturbated into aforementioned socks and left them in the back of the closet for a month. Needless to say, my generation's anthem didn't make a whole lot of sense to me at the time lyrically, yet it still managed to move all of us collectively in this new, powerfully unbridled way. Maybe that was the point.

The changes happening in music were a perfect mirror to my own personal transformation. My cassette tape collection pre-1991 was dominated by the hair metal bands of the era, in all their macho makeup and frilly leather-clad glory: Def Leppard, Poison, Mötley Crüe and their countless other finely coiffed cohorts. There was a lot of talk about "partying" and looking back, an alarming amount of references to under-aged girls. Most of it was silly gibberish to me at the time considering I had at this point never even attended a party, let alone partaken in the verb form of the word.

Parallel to all the glitz and glam of the hair bands and before grunge really took off in earnest, there was the rise of hip hop—or at least it's introduction into my sheltered, suburban world. In truth, rap was more of a curiosity for me in those years. As a white kid in Catholic school, there were only a few, highly-sought-after but always elusive mix tapes floating around, usually smuggled onto the playground at recess by that one kid with the older brother in high school.

You know the kid. He's the same dude who had the Vanna White issue of *Playboy* in his backpack and chugged one of his dad's O'Douls at lunch. There were a lot of awkward times with that kid.

These mix tapes were usually a grab-bag of songs with no apparent connection other than the repeated use of the holy grail of swear words: Fuck. Even as a grown man, it still feels a little spicy dropping that one in writing. So you can imagine my rebellious joy to hear that and a litany of other new-to-me expletives chanted over and over again. It was delightfully deviant.

Looking back as an adult, I can clearly see the massive divide between the usage and sentiment in NWA's *Fuck the Police* compared to 2 Live Crew's *Face Down Ass Up* (the chorus of course echoing "that's the way we like to fuck"). Same word. Same giggles from fourteen-year-old me. Very different meanings. Not that I would have really understood either.

Most of my impressions of law enforcement up to this point came from either the *Police Academy* movies or the TV show *Chips*. If you ask me, that's about as textbook white privilege as it gets. At the time, I had no real concept of the disturbing and extreme dichotomy of my childhood compared to the young men in the songs I was listening to.

As for 2 Live Crew's opus on preferred sexual positions, I wasn't even sure how the logistics of the whole penis-in-vagina thing worked, let alone that there were optional alignments to consider. I was also still pretty sure touching a boob would feel like one big muscle. I had a lot to learn.

Needless to say, hip hop felt a little too mature for me in those days. Any time I'd listen to rap it was like I was sneaking into a high school party and hiding behind a house plant, hoping to not get discovered. I had no idea what the older kids around me were talking about but desperately wanted to be cool enough to be part of the conversation.

But once I heard the new flannel-clad flood of energy coming out of Seattle, my connection to music changed forever. Culturally, Nirvana was the definitive tip of the spear. But personally, it was Pearl Jam's *Ten* that would be the cornerstone of my first few truly powerful musical experiences.

While famously not the most well-enunciated singer, listening to Eddie Vedder belt out *Alive* was the first time a song nearly brought me to tears while simultaneously making the hairs on my arm stand up. I *felt* what he was saying more than I *knew* what he was saying, which left this beautifully open space for personal interpretation.

The lyrics loosely detail a conversation where a mother tells her son that the person he knew as his father wasn't really biologically related to him and all the while his real father was dying. It also calls out the son's age as thirteen. I was fourteen at the time and adopted. To say this struck a chord is an injustice of simplicity.

As the anthem of the chorus swells, Eddie repeats "I'm still alive" over and over again. There's truth in that refrain that still resonates with me some twenty-five years later, usually ending in me digging through old boxes buried in the back of a closet in search of flannel shirts, thermal underwear and a pair of Dr. Martens.

It's usually around this same age that Catholic school students go through the sacrament of Confirmation. And it makes sense given all this new-found independence and choice. The ceremony is essentially a re-affirming of your faith as someone who is approaching adulthood, like a lot of the "welcome to the club" rites of passage found in other religions.

In theory, I think it's an inspiring and beautiful gesture. I imagine most people are born into their religion, so there's not a lot of choice involved. But by recognizing those early feelings of empowerment that often come with the first few years of adolescence, it seems like a healthy way to embrace the religion on your own terms. *In theory.*

Except here's the thing—I made horrible decisions all the time at fourteen. I seriously had no business being behind the wheel of my own life with all the hormones that were raging through me. And I had a boner, like, twenty-three hours a day. I was pretty much all instinct and urges, all the time. There was very little deep, thoughtful analysis going on. Oh, and did I mention the boners?

Part of my homework for Confirmation included picking a patron saint, which would then be my "Confirmation name." If I remember correctly, the guidance from my teacher was something along the lines of "choose a saint that will serve as your inspiration and guide in living a holy life."

I chose St. Anthony. As in Anthony Kiedis of the Red Hot Chili Peppers. From what I knew, he apparently spent a lot of time under bridges which seemed like a saintly thing to do. Plus, he had some really rad tattoos.

See? Horrible decisions (no offense to Mr. Kiedis). And someone expects me to judiciously pick which team I will be on in this epic battle of "who guessed the afterlife correctly?"

Keep in mind, I don't know the first thing about other Christian religions, let alone teams in the other leagues. The extent of my spiritual exploration up to this point was a brief conversation with the older next-door neighbor girl whose family happened to be Lutheran. Other than some debate about how much of a fuss to make over Jesus' mother Mary, it didn't seem all that different.

If the Catholic church wanted to get really progressive—which is of course what it's known for—they would invite other religions in for a Faith Career Fair just before Confirmation. I imagine it would be a lot like those crowded, sweaty college gymnasiums filled with booths for Enterprise Rent-A-Car, State Farm Insurance and Chase Bank. There would be a table for Buddhism, Islam, Hinduism, Judaism, maybe even Scientology for good measure.

Of course, the Greek Gods would be sulking in the hallway because for the 2,000th year in a row no one sent them the registration form and they're starting to think they're no longer being taken seriously.

It feels like it would be an enlightening experience walking the room, shaking some hands, reading pamphlets, setting up interviews, picking up little swag items at each booth (rumor has it the Rastafarians are giving out brownies).

In all seriousness, it's hard for me to look at organized religions as a whole and see much more than different versions of people claiming to have a map of what Shakespeare referred to as *the undiscovered country*. Kind of like that recruiter that offered you six-figures within your first two years out of college; it sounds great but more than likely it's a pyramid scheme.

What I'm saying is I didn't exactly try on a lot of other hats before signing an extended deal with the Catholics. It was kind of like voting in a country run by a dictator. Technically I voted but there was only one name on the ballot.

Not only is this decision happening right as puberty is kicking in and with very little knowledge of the other options, but as a student in a Catholic school, saying no or choosing another team would have meant turning away from everyone and everything I knew. At this point, both my grandparents were still alive, so there was the added issue that anything other than an enthusiastic "yes, please" would feel like I was letting them down, which was a fate far worse than eternal damnation.

So I'm decidedly in the "yes" column for this whole Confirmation thing and I've picked St. Anthony of Chili Peppers as my patron saint. That means the final item on the to-do list is choosing a sponsor.

This was one of the many times where it was great having an older sibling; I regularly got a preview of things to come in my own biography. And not unlike most younger siblings, I thought the world of my big sister. So logically, whatever trail she blazed seemed like a safe path to follow. She also had the first-round draft pick for Confirmation sponsors, rightfully using it to select our grandmother a few years earlier—who was essentially a living embodiment of the faith. Never one to stray too far from the roads my sister paved, I was planning to ask my grandfather to be my sponsor.

To be clear, the role isn't nearly as prestigious as it might sound. Essentially, the person stands next to you during mass and you walk up to the priest together, everyone says some magic words and then we all head home for cake.

But there were some complications. My grandfather's health had started to decline rapidly and along with needing to carry an oxygen tank along with him, he was starting to suffer from the early stages of what would later be diagnosed as Alzheimer's. We just weren't sure he was up for it.

When I finally mustered the courage to ask, he was all aglow. It was like someone jabbed him in the soul with an epi pen and he burst back to life. Looking back, for all the foolish decisions I made at that age, there are a handful I'm still pretty proud of— with this one near the top. It may have also been the first time I realized that a seemingly small act on my part could be a very big deal to someone who loved me as much as he did.

The big day comes and our family heads to the Old Cathedral in downtown St. Louis. Say what you will about the inherent corruption, misogyny and general hypocrisy of the Catholic church as an organization—they definitely know how to build some breathtaking architecture.

But here's the thing with these grand buildings: they're meant to make the people inside feel small. It's a brilliant piece of psychological propaganda. Step into one of those older churches and you instantly feel like you're humbled before the grandeur of it all. You can palpably feel your smallness before the great and powerful Oz.

There's not much I remember about the service or the day on

the whole, except for a brief moment of what I can only describe as *complimentary racism*. We were near the end of mass and at the point where all the Confirmation candidates and their sponsors line up in a procession toward the front of the church. As we approached the altar, each student stopped in front of the bishop and recited a sort of Holy Pledge of Allegiance.

I nailed this bit and my grandfather and I walked back triumphantly to our seats. As we sat down, after what was a beautiful moment of bonding, my grandfather leans in and says to me, in a soft and gentle tone, "That's the nicest colored man I've ever met."

I was speechless and really confused about some seriously conflicting emotions. I think I mumbled a response that was something like "Uh, yeah." But inside, I was really ashamed. And confused.

I loved my grandfather deeply and while his sentiment was intended as a compliment, it was also the ugly byproduct of generations of institutionalized discrimination, prejudice and bias. That cultural divide and sense of "otherness" was so deep he didn't even have the vocabulary to simply say, "That was one of the nicest priests I've ever met."

There I am, literally minutes after becoming an official, fully-fledged member of the JC fan club and I'm already at a moral crossroads. Is this some sort of divine pop quiz? Is this going to be happening regularly now to keep me on my toes?

I was certain racism was a big sin and it was my duty as a

Christian to stand up and say or do something, no matter where it came from. That magic book everyone in the church was always going on about definitely had a part explaining that we were all made in the "image and likeness of God." I don't remember seeing any disclaimers about skin color.

But this felt complicated. It was a compliment—and also a completely unnecessary mention of the priest's race.

Even today talking about race with older, white relatives is a sensitive topic I approach with extreme caution, not being nearly as courageous as I'd hope to be. It usually feels like I'm picking my battles using some sort of internal racist Geiger counter. Anything registering over 500 and I don't care if I ruin Thanksgiving dinner, I'm saying something.

But back then, at fourteen, I was all knees and elbows— physically, emotionally and intellectually—and nowhere near brave enough to speak up in the moment. So I said "Uh, yeah" and stared at my shoes. Not my proudest moment and I hope I haven't let too many since then pass by unchecked. But if I'm being honest, I'm pretty sure I was just trying to make it through the day so I could get back to playing *Lakers vs. Celtics* on my Sega Genesis.

INTRODUCING THE FUTURE
MR. ALYSSA MILANO

Since most of the Catholic elementary schools in St. Louis only had about twenty to thirty students in each grade, it left little opportunity for those same students to interact with someone of the opposite sex who hadn't also been a classmate for the past eight years. And that suited me just fine. I had my own battles I was fighting.

Once I hit puberty and had all these new hormones pumping through my veins, I was in a constant state of contradiction. Biologically, I wanted to masturbate *all the time*. But my brain had been taught that God was watching everything I did and could even read my mind. My thoughts were supposed to be "untainted."

Ironically, I didn't know enough about sex or the female body to even fantasize correctly had I wanted to. It was all a mental collage of mostly covered-up boobs and butts that I'd seen in the lingerie section of the Sears catalog. For the record, that might explain why I've still got a thing for old lady bras. But that's a whole other story I don't think anyone ever needs to read.

When I first entered puberty, masturbation wasn't really about wanting to have sex or be physically intimate in any way with someone else—the more pressing concern was figuring out how my own newly-upgraded equipment worked. I was perfectly happy being a one-man show.

I was a late-bloomer when it came to dating but thankfully was planted in a field full of late-bloomers. It didn't feel particularly unusual that I entered high school without ever having really kissed a girl. That's not to say I hadn't started to notice girls in that way—I was very much "girl crazy," as demonstrated by my decision to swap the Bo Jackson poster on my bedroom door with one of teen queen Alyssa Milano.

This new addition to my room, mind you, was about as tame as it gets. The classic poster featured a young Ms. Milano in an oversized New Jersey Devils hockey jersey and a pair of jeans that had a hole over one knee, exposing the slightest bit of flesh a few inches above her kneecap. I was crushing hard. But despite all my overactive hormones, this new interest wasn't really about sex, per se—it was about romance. I thought she was really cute and was mostly daydreaming about holding hands with her at the mall while we walked to Sbarro for a romantic dinner.

And I was starting to have those thoughts about other girls, too. If that meant I was going to have to go through Tony Danza, so be it.

In addition to the co-ed Catholic schools like the one I attended, beginning in junior high, there was the added option to transfer to an all-boys or all-girls school, which served as a sort of feeder program into the high school they shared a building with. In order to facilitate proper socialization (whatever that meant), these mono-gendered schools would hold "mixers" that were essentially early versions of a high school dance without the pressure of bringing a date. Kids from the surrounding Catholic schools would sign up to attend, dressed to the nines in their best gear, drenched in Calvin Klein cologne and Rave hairspray.

I was particularly excited about the preening and costuming involved. It was just another form of dress-up. And since it was the early nineties—during the brief window of time where MC Hammer pants were worn unironically—I use the term *fashion* very loosely when describing the clothes that were in my closet.

Nevertheless, for me and my friends nothing said cool quite like Z Cavaricci.

The absurdly high-waisted pants came with an equally absurdly-thin belt, usually made from a texture meant to imitate some sort of reptile. The more fashionable versions of these pants came with multiple belts, positioned like a stack of Swatch watches on a wrist, each with its own shiny silver buckle.

But the real trademark was the white tag that ran down the

front of the zipper with the letters Z-C-A-V-A-R-I-C-C-I stacked vertically down the label. That was how you knew it was legit. Too legit, in fact, to quit.

The problem with this latest fashion trend was that each pair of pants costs something like $80. That price tag put them well out of reach for anything I'd ever be able to convince my parents to buy for me and I was far too impatient with my own money to save up enough to buy them myself. If I made it a full twenty-four hours without spending any cash I had on CDs and baseball cards, it was an act of divine intervention.

Fortunately for working-class families like mine there was a knock-off version that sold for about half the price. Cleverly branded as Code Zero, the pants looked nearly identical to the premium version, including the white tag on the zipper. When written vertically in all caps, it created a sort of optical illusion where CODEZERO kind of looked like ZCAVARICCI from a distance. There was a C and Z, so close enough.

To really complete the look, the pant legs needed to be "tight-rolled" at the ankles. This was a delicate procedure, involving first grabbing about an inch of fabric between your thumb and forefinger and then folding it over horizontally, while quickly taking the remainder of the cuff and rolling it up vertically. You knew you'd gotten it right if you could no longer feel your feet and your toes had started to turn purple.

It's recently come to my attention that this trend seems to have returned; I'm nostalgically nauseous.

The tight-rolled slacks of course were only half the outfit. The top was just as important and there were a few big decisions to make right from the beginning: t-shirt or button down. If I went the t-shirt route, it had to be at least two sizes too big. And it couldn't just be a plain t-shirt, either. There needed to be some kind of large branded logo on it that was big enough to be seen from space.

Tommy Hilfiger, Nautica and even FUBU were among my favorites, until one day I saw on *YO! MTV RAPS* that FUBU meant *For Us By Us* and I was understandably not part of that "us." It wasn't so much an attempt at cultural appropriation as it was an uninformed, sheltered white kid in Catholic school who thought the logo looked really cool and didn't know any better.

The oversized t-shirts were all well and good but an event as important as a mixer required the big guns. That meant any number of silk floral-patterned button-down shirts that somehow featured bright, vivid colors and drab earth-tones all at the same time. And because nothing in the early nineties was actually supposed to fit correctly, I guess my thinking was that these oversized, flowing shirts would accentuate the fluidity of my dance moves while doing the cabbage patch or electric slide. Granted, I didn't have the slightest idea how to do either of those (or any) dances but figured if I ever learned, it was a good idea to already have the right clothing for it.

These mixers were the first in what would be a long line of social gatherings that were heavily biased toward those majestic extroverts brave enough to navigate the dance floor. It was practice for the many sketchy nightclubs I would be forced to navigate in my adult years with the hopes of finding a mate, be it temporarily or otherwise. Except this early version didn't even serve drinks.

It was all pretty dreadful, but I had no other means of meeting girls from other schools—and they were all out on the dance floor seemingly having the time of their lives.

I've always been a disaster on the dance floor, even by white guy standards. As you may have guessed, I have a bit of trouble getting out of my head and "into my body" as my more rhythmically gifted friends might say. For me, dancing is a very unnatural activity, so I feel like I have to really think about what I'm doing and the second my brain gets involved, it's game over. I get incredibly self-conscious and suddenly feel like I need to voluntarily control motor functions that just moments earlier seemed to work fine on their own.

Under normal circumstances, while I'm walking down the street I'm not thinking "and left foot, now right foot, and left again . . ." but once I'm dancing it's like all my limbs suddenly need constant instructions. It's a troubling experience and at times I worry if I stay too long on the dance floor, other previously involuntary body parts will start requiring focus as well. One song too many and I might have to intentionally concentrate on keeping my small intestine working. It's just too dangerous.

I knew I had to be on the dance floor, though. Those boys along the wall and in the bleachers were never getting a girl's phone number, which of course was the whole point of the evening. So instead of joining the wallflowers, I would walk this sort of patrol route, zig-zagging through the crowd like I was perpetually taking a quick break to use the bathroom or looking for my group of friends.

As I'm sure you can guess, those friends didn't exist and that bathroom visit never happened. But I felt like I had to be active and dancing was out of the question, so in my mind this was the middle ground. I would simply repeat my route over and over again throughout the evening until the music stopped.

In the rare case I had actually caught the eye of a nice young lady and managed to somehow attempt a conversation, the music was usually so loud that I could only make out every fourth or fifth word she said. Sadly, this too would prove to be foreshadowing of many more years of failed attempts at talking to women in bars and clubs. It was conversational *Mad Libs*.

The typical interaction would go something like this:

"Hi . . . what . . . name . . . go . . . escalator," the cute girl with the neon green headband would seemingly say, glowing like an angel in between the flashes of strobe lights.

"I'm sorry, did you just say *escalator?*" I would reply, losing all but 25% of my intended question to the bass bellowing from the oversized speakers in the corner of the gymnasium.

"... did ... say ... respirator?" she would respond.

Needless to say, it was a very rare occasion that I ever ended up dancing with someone. Eventually, the music would begin to die down and I would make my way through the crowd to the front door, where my dad would be waiting to pick me up in our rusted-out white 1977 Monte Carlo that looked more like a seafaring vessel than an automobile. I would embarrassingly climb into the beast of a vehicle with little to show for the evening other than a few new sweat stains on my oversized black and beige paisley-print shirt.

But damn did I look good.

IS YOUR REFRIGERATOR RUNNING?

The holy grail of interacting with the opposite sex during junior high was getting a girl's phone number. And while I didn't exactly have the highest batting average, I did get a number or two in my day. Like a solar eclipse, it was rare and required some extraordinary circumstances, but it did happen on occasion, usually requiring some sort of specialized viewing device to avoid any permanent retinal damage. And since I was growing up in a time long before texting, that meant I had to actually talk on the phone if I wanted to get to know someone. It was miserable.

Like the three or four generations before me, I grew up in an era where landline phones dominated social communication. Personally, I've always found the devices to be a rather rude and invasive form of technology, blaring unexpectedly like a child throwing a temper tantrum at the dinner table while the adults try to have a civilized conversation. Each annoying ring feels like some spoiled brat's pleas for attention: "Stop what you're doing right now and listen to me!"

Since my family didn't have an answering machine until I was in high school, there wasn't the option of setting the ringer to mute and screening calls. My parents apparently felt we needed to be available 24/7 in case President Reagan called looking for advice on ending the Cold War with Gorbachev.

There was one instance, and one instance only, where I welcomed the sound of the phone ringing and that was when there had been a decent snowfall the night before. If the lawn was comfortably tucked away under a blanket of white when I woke up and the phone rang before 8:00 a.m., it usually meant school was canceled. It was pure joy.

The closest equivalent to that sensation I've experienced as an adult is having someone cancel plans at the last minute. I play it off all calm and neutral on the outside, offering an empathetic "Yeah, I totally understand. No, nothing to be sorry about. Yes, of course, let's get something on the calendar soon. I'll text you." But on the inside, I just got a snow day. I'm absolutely thrilled as I bar and lock the doors to my fortress of solitude and vanish into whatever gloriously solo activities I'll end up occupying myself with for the evening.

In the eternal war of introverts vs. extroverts, there seems to be a natural ebb and flow to who is winning the battle of communication technology. And to be fair, my fellow introverts and I have historically been at an advantage. For thousands of years, letter writing was obviously the main way people would communicate over distance. As you might imagine, that's my sweet spot.

I'm usually not particularly witty in the moment. If I have an interesting conversation with someone at a dinner party, I'm not really bringing my A-game while we're talking. It won't be until a day or so later when I'm grocery shopping that I think up the perfect personal anecdote that would have played wonderfully in the moment. Even then, it takes another two or three edits before it's even close to resembling something witty or insightful. I usually need to swing a few times before I make contact and trying to edit while in the middle of a conversation can be cumbersome, to say the least.

~

In our family there were only three phones in the house. There was one in my parent's bedroom but that was typically off-limits. Then there was the main family phone in the kitchen, hanging right next to the doorway leading to the living room, providing the slightest bit of room-to-room mobility thanks to the extra-long cord that for some unknown reason was coiled to resemble a never-ending curly fry.

Last but not least was the phone next to the bar in our partially-finished basement. The bar itself was an ancient relic of my parents' seemingly active social life pre-children. At one point in time, the onyx-colored slab of wood stocked with liquor bottles and assorted glassware allowed my dad to live out his fantasy of being a bartender, serving up Vodka Gimlets and Gin & Tonics to the mostly plaid-panted, turtleneck-wearing patrons of his personal establishment.

But by the time I came around, it had long since been reduced to little more than a glorified table, holding any excess of dry goods we had on hand, buried under bags of chips, twelve-packs of paper towels and assorted canned vegetables. That was the one phone in the house where there was a semblance of privacy, making it the best spot by far for calling girls.

Maybe it's aftershocks from my preteen years that continue to rumble and cause the occasional tremor but I still get butterflies in my stomach if I have to call someone on the phone. In those earliest years, the anxiety was crippling. It didn't help that I had no idea who would answer the phone if I ever had the courage to call.

Meeting a romantic partner's parents is stressful enough once you've been dating for a while but using these barbaric landlines meant I could be greeted by the deep, intimidating voice of the girl's father before I'd even spoken a word to her. A trial by fire is one thing but this was getting tossed directly into a volcano as a human sacrifice.

Only slightly less terrifying was the possibility of one of her siblings answering the phone. Brothers were usually the worst, generally being the blunter and more oafish of the sexes. But I could usually anticipate the verbal wedgie that was about to happen and brace myself accordingly. It was typically a simple interrogation involving a few rounds of questioning about who I was and why I was calling, with the sole intention of getting under my skin. If I failed, they simply hung up and I was left to try again another time, hoping for better odds.

If I managed to appease the sibling's inquiries, it was inevitably followed by them calling out their sister's name at top volume. "Heather! The phones for you," they would holler. "It's a booooooooooy!" This added bit of detail was completely unnecessary in my mind and only served to further tense up every muscle in my face until it was contorted into a form usually only seen in funhouse mirrors.

Mothers, on the other hand, tended to be much gentler about the whole thing. There was usually a sentimentality in their voice, though it often came across sounding like they were talking to a toddler or a puppy. It was as if they wanted to take a Polaroid of the moment and hang it on the fridge with the label "first phone call from a boy."

In the off chance the girl I was hoping to talk to actually answered the phone herself, I was usually so in shock that my charming and well-rehearsed lead-in would deteriorate into about five seconds of awkward silence like some prank call gone wrong.

"Is . . . your . . . refrigerator running?" It was a disaster.

"Is this some sort of crank call?" the sweet but suspicious young lady on the other end would reply.

"Oh, ummm no. Sorry. We met at the mixer last weekend?" I would squeak like a mouse caught in a trap.

Mentally psyching myself up to get past her guardians left me ill-prepared to actually speak to her directly. If she answered the phone herself, especially within the first few rings, it was a curveball that almost always led to a swing and a miss on my part.

$$\sim$$

Those earliest attempts at conversation were painful, to say the least. My self-esteem wasn't nearly high enough to deal with not being able to look someone in the face or read their body language—you can't hear someone smile or roll their eyes. And the inevitable silences left me stumbling. So much so that after a few truly disastrous attempts at maintaining a coherent conversation, I started writing outlines of some key topics, questions or clever quips I could work in.

It went about as well as you'd imagine, more often than not sounding like an odd mutation of Tourette syndrome where my nervous tick was shouting out random, unrelated bits of small talk without context or waiting for a reply.

"Weather, huh?"

"Do you school?"

"What's your favorite musics?"

Assuming I somehow managed to get the girl on the other end to stay on the line, there was one more obstacle in my way: privacy. All it took for someone else to listen in on the call was to pick up a receiver in another room. Convenient when both grandma and grandpa want to wish you a happy birthday at the same time but dangerous when in the wrong hands.

It was essentially a form of wiretapping, a fact not lost on the clever girls I knew. There was a particularly sneaky bit of espionage where one of the girl's friends would call under the guise of information gathering. Little did I know, but the girl I liked would be listening in on the other side as well, quietly waiting in the wings as her friend investigated whether I liked her or *liked* liked her.

It was all quite brilliant, if not a bit deceptive. But it did little to ease my paranoia about talking on the phone.

Today, things have clearly swung back in favor of the introverts as the internet, apps, texting and email have taken over as the way most of us connect with one another. And while both text and email come with their own challenges, mostly around passive-aggressively misinterpreting tone—*per your last email*—there is at least some level of authorship where I can compulsively edit as much as my neurotic heart desires before the message reaches its intended audience.

I can only hope that I'm long dead and gone by the time the tides shift again in favor of the extroverts and whatever invasive technology they'll unleash upon the world next. When neurological implants become popular, letting people telepathically send a message to someone's brain directly, you can count me out. It's crowded enough in my mind as is. I don't need the extra company.

HIDE & SEEK

Dating in high school, at least for the first few years, was something other people did that I just sort of observed from a safe distance. Kind of like how I view scuba diving today. I can see the appeal and it does look like fun once you're down in the water doing pirouettes with the dolphins and all that, but I don't have the slightest idea how someone gets into it initially.

Do you have to buy all the gear yourself? Do you take classes? Do you have to be a strong swimmer? What do you do if you don't live by the ocean? It seems like a big initial investment and given my proclivity for changing my mind before so much as even touching the water, I wouldn't want to buy all the stuff only to discover I'd really rather just watch a Netflix documentary on deep-sea diving.

Except—you know—with dating.

Entering high school meant a whole new group of wonderful young women that I'm sure would have made great first girlfriends, but unless one of them walked right up to me, took me by the hand and said "You are now my boyfriend," there was little chance I was actually going to ask any of them out. And while some of that was simple inexperience, a lot of it was the fact I was really bad at reading signs. Unfortunately, I'm still atrocious at this; the subtle art of flirtation is all but lost on me.

But it wasn't just miscommunication that was standing in my way. I had a pretty packed schedule. As I experienced it, the "popular jock" trope that's become a staple of Hollywood high school movies is a myth. I played three varsity sports in high school and that meant year-long practices and training in the offseason. And I took it all extremely seriously. I was very aware from a young age of my family's financial situation and that if I was going to go to college I would need a scholarship to help pay for it. That meant while my friends were up in the stands actually learning how to talk to girls, I was on the field or the court or the track very much *not* talking to girls.

On the weekends, I was working. If I wanted money to buy that new Pixies CD, I was going to have to earn it. I got my first official paycheck when I was fourteen, working at the same neighborhood bagel shop as my older sister before me. Saturday and Sunday mornings were spent schlepping sesame seed bagels to the predominately older, Jewish clientele. It was a painless gig that funded my frequent visits to the record store down the street.

My first job was also a small but critical step out of the homogeneous white Catholic culture I inhabited during the rest of the week. Interestingly enough, one of the first words I ever learned in a language other than English was *goyim*, followed shortly thereafter with *schmuck*. When you're a teenager, dick jokes know no cultural or linguistic borders.

It's probably not a huge surprise that when it was time for my first homecoming dance, I was in no way prepared to find a date. I'd only been in high school a few months and most of the girls I knew were classmates in the "advanced" courses I was taking—I had guessed correctly enough times on the placement tests to somehow get lumped in with the smart kids. As you might imagine, we weren't the most socially adventurous bunch and there wasn't a lot of Alyssa-Milano-in-a-hockey-jersey level chemistry happening on my end.

But behind the scenes, my football coach Father Mark had been plotting with my older sister—who was a senior at the same school—to set me up with someone. That someone, it turns out, was my sister's boyfriend's younger sister. Yeah, it's as clunky and awkward reading that as it was in real life.

While I appreciated the gesture from my well-meaning

matchmakers, even at the time it seemed a little lazy. Kind of like realizing you forgot to buy a present for a holiday gift exchange then frantically scurrying around the house for something you can pass off as a gift. They had decided to wrap up the first thing they could find, giving me the remote control for the TV.

Despite what I may have perceived as a lack of effort on the part of my sister and the priest, I was genuinely thankful for the assistance. But this poor girl was in an even worse predicament than I was. She had to go to the dance with me and I *definitely* didn't want to be there.

It wasn't a bad match on paper; she was also a three-sport athlete and there was that whole bit about our siblings dating. But the biggest thing we shared in common was that neither of us were any good at talking to the opposite sex. And while she was a beautiful young woman, I couldn't shake the fact she looked like her brother in a blonde wig.

To be clear, that's not a slight to her— that's my own unique brand of weird issues popping up. Since both my older sister and I were adopted, I wasn't used to family members that looked so much alike. My sister and I can pass as siblings in the sense we're both generically Caucasian, but we don't really have the same facial features or mannerisms.

The dance went about as you'd imagine, with moments of awkwardness so intense we probably both immediately purged them from our memory. I'm sure we ended the evening with a hug or possibly even a stout handshake and then proceeded to never speak to one another again. Not out of bitterness or any sort of malice—we simply had different groups of friends, were in different classes and had busy athletic schedules.

That is until about a month later when we were both invited to the same party.

To be fair, it was less of a party and more a small group of people hanging out at someone's house who all happened to be there at the same time. If memory serves, there were four girls and four boys, and we were all sitting in the basement watching *Wayne's World*. After the movie, one of the girls recommended we play hide and seek.

It seemed a little childish at the time, but I was pretty new to the whole socializing with girls thing, so I figured maybe it was just some sort of fun icebreaker. The girl who suggested the idea proceeded to turn off the lights, instructed everyone to go hide and then started counting backward from twenty.

Like the good rule-follower I was, I hurried off to the other side of the basement where I saw what looked like a pantry door. I stealthily crammed myself inside and proceeded to do the best hiding I could manage. About ten minutes later, I noticed things were still unusually quiet.

I was pretty proud of my sneaky hiding spot, but it wasn't *that* good. I gave it about another five minutes before giving up and heading back to the main TV area. On my way, I heard what sounded like an awful lot of lip smacking going on behind one of the couches. A few feet further off and it sounded like someone was wrestling around on the floor. I was so innocently naïve that it wasn't until I nearly walked into a pair of my friends making out that I realized what was going on. My face immediately flushed so intensely bright red that I'm pretty sure you could see it glowing in the dark.

I made my way back to the couch where we had been watching TV and there was my homecoming date from a few weeks earlier, sitting arms crossed. I offered up a meager "So . . . I guess we're not playing hide and seek?" while trying to cling to what little shred of dignity I had left. She remained silent as a stone and nearly motionless with the exception of what appeared to be a tiny half-smile. As quickly as it appeared, it went away and her and I spent the rest of the evening watching *Melrose Place* in silence while our friends swapped saliva in the background.

For the record, I feel like I won our little game of hide and seek, even if it was on account of a technicality. Yeah—I'm definitely counting it.

REBEL WITHOUT A CAR

I got my driver's license halfway through my sophomore year of high school. That little plastic card was my first real taste of independence and would be the doorway to a whole new world of experiences. Or so I had convinced myself.

While many of my classmates' sixteenth birthdays included keys to a shiny new car, I would be inheriting a Ford Tempo that was nearly as old as I was. Don't get me wrong—it was considerably better than continuing to carpool and since I only had to pay for gas, I was thankful for the hand-me-down.

At one point in time the dark gray economy sedan had been my father's car, then for a brief stint my older sister was behind the wheel before finally passing it on to me. And while the bass from the speakers wouldn't exactly be shaking the windows any time soon, the car did have a cassette player, which was a big upgrade for me at the time. The ability to listen to music of my own choosing—and even make special road trip mix tapes—was nearly as freeing as actually being able to go places on my own.

For years, there were two options when traveling in a car with my family: silence or the local oldies station KLOU that played saccharine-drenched pop songs from the fifties and sixties. To this day, hearing Chubby Checker's *The Twist* triggers a Pavlovian response that makes my mouth start to water as if I'm about to throw up.

Which is to say I was pretty convinced both my parents had lousy taste in music—along with most things that required any sense of artistic value, as demonstrated by the drab, velvety faux-art that littered the walls of our house. And while I applaud them for seemingly having hired a blind interior decorator who selected the various gloomy landscape portraits based on texture rather than composition, it left our home looking like a funeral parlor.

The one exception to this artistic rule was my dad's unexpected fondness for the music of Chuck Berry. Maybe it was the shared connection to St. Louis, but Chuck was one of the only musicians that stirred any kind of reaction from my father. Being the generally muted person that he was, that reaction was usually limited to a low rumbling "all-riiiiiight" as *Johnny B. Goode*, *Maybellene* or *Roll Over Beethoven* came on the radio.

One of my fondest memories of spending time with my father as an adult was when I took him to see Mr. Berry play at a small club in St. Louis called Blueberry Hill. I was living in Chicago at the time and my visits back home were rare, so during those trips I made a point of dragging my retired father out of his comfort zone and the sedentary life that had become so familiar to him.

The show ended up being unexpectedly sentimental for me when I realized Chuck would be performing with his own son, Charles Berry Jr.

Chuck's ongoing battle with arthritis made it difficult for him to play for an extended period of time and the beautifully elegant solution was his son playing lead guitar for most of the show, gently fading into the background as his dad did his legendary "duck walk." It was a powerful parallel to the experience I was having with my own father.

But on my sixteenth birthday, my only interest was annoying my dad enough that he would bring me to the DMV to get my license as soon as humanly possible. Despite not even attempting the parallel parking portion of the exam, I somehow managed to pass on my first attempt.

Looking back, the lack of parallel parking was a bit short-sighted on my part. My world was pretty small at the time and I rarely ventured beyond the boundaries of suburbia, where between the easily available residential street parking and what seemed to be naturally occurring paved parking lots, my driving skills were seldom put to the test. I would be in for a pretty big surprise the first time I found the courage to drive "in the city."

A mere twenty-four hours after getting my license, I was ready to test the boundaries of this new freedom. In what I initially envisioned playing out like a scene from *The Fresh Prince of Bel-Air*, I was dead set on skipping homeroom that morning thanks to my new vehicular-inspired independence.

I had no plan other than not being at school and in what would end up being a pretty lame attempt at rebellion, I simply drove to the Dunkin Donuts down the street from my high school. I didn't care much for coffee and wasn't particularly enthusiastic about donuts, but it was close to the school and had a parking lot, so it seemed like an obvious candidate for my mini-adventure.

The problems arose when I went to leave. I had intentionally parked in a spot with vacancies to either side, thinking there was no sense in pushing my luck. I scarfed down an éclair and a small, single-serving carton of orange juice before making my way back to my car, only to discover my vehicle now had two new neighbors.

On the list of maneuvers requiring a high level of skill from the driver, backing out of a parking spot doesn't rank particularly high. But I've always struggled with geometry and somehow got the angle wrong. The bumper of my car gently brushed up against the door of the beige Volvo beside me. As luck would have it, the car's owner was returning just in time to witness the entire debacle.

Nearly in tears, I apologized as sincerely as I could and explained my predicament with hands shaking. The well-dressed middle-aged woman—who's car had just been sideswiped—was kind, patient and clearly a parent herself. She took down my information but promised that if her husband could remove the scuff marks there wouldn't be any need to let our insurance companies in on the incident.

On one condition: I had to tell my parents what happened. At 8:35 a.m. on a Tuesday, I found myself on a payphone explaining to my father that I had just been in my first fender-bender a mere day after getting my license.

I think he was initially in shock at the audacity it took to even consider skipping school literally the first opportunity I got. Any concern about the actual accident was secondary. His most frequent observation of my often-ill-fated teenage behavior was that he "couldn't understand how a kid so smart could act so dumb all the damn time." And he was right.

It was like someone had handed me a newborn baby chick— with the clear instructions to hold it gently—and as soon as it was in my palm I clenched my hand into a fist. "Chicky dead? No . . . chicky just sleeping. Nice chicky." These were clearly not going to be my wisest years.

THE THREE-STRIKE SHUFFLE

I grew up in what my dad would proudly describe as a "sports family." As soon as we were old enough, he put us in just about every athletic activity our school offered. Granted, those first few years involved little more than tee-ball and a devolved form of soccer that looked more like a herd of goats than a team sport. Imagine a field full of eighties "bowl" haircuts merging into this sort of amoeba-like mass of uncoordinated little feet, all unified in the chaotic chase of some black and white ball. It was instant entropy at the sound of a whistle.

In general, I didn't mind the year-round athletic schedule my dad signed us up for, with one glaring exception: baseball. It was the bane of my existence growing up. The fact that I was horrible at it probably didn't help.

From an early age, I was described by teammates as "that kid who throws like a girl." Except they were dead wrong. Both of my sisters were excellent softball players and they could throw a ball way better than me, so in my mind saying I "threw like a girl" wasn't so much an insult as it was a simple misclassification. I'd seen girls throw and I *definitely* didn't throw like a girl. I threw like someone who had no interest whatsoever in playing baseball.

Perhaps the bigger issue was the fact that I could barely see the ball. I've had horrible eyesight for as long as I can remember but it wasn't until I finally got contacts in college that I really had a grasp of just how bad my vision had been as a kid. The first time I was able to recognize someone waving at me from across the university's cafeteria felt like I had acquired some sort of new superpower. It was HD before HD was a thing.

There was instantly a dramatic decrease in the number of times I'd enthusiastically wave back to strangers who had intended their greeting for the person behind me. That's not to say it stopped happening, just that the frequency was lower. Over the years I've come to terms with the fact I'm a magnet for awkward encounters. Just last week I tried to fist bump the gas station attendant who was simply reaching for my debit card. He was just as confused as I was, but thankfully played along.

✺

My parents recognized something wasn't quite right with my vision when I was around six years old and we were driving to visit relatives on the other side of the Mississippi river. There's this spot as you cross the bridge where you can begin to make out the shape of the Arch and it was tradition for someone in the car to call it out. It was our own little modified version of *I Spy*.

I was pretty terrible at our game. But like most kids with a physical difficulty, I learned to adapt and fake it. I was excellent at getting second place in our little sightseeing challenge, despite the fact it wasn't exactly celebrated—or even acknowledged— by the other family members in the car. Undeterred, once the first person would triumphantly announce that they had spotted the giant silver half-of-a-McDonald's-sign in the distance, I would instantly chime in with a well-placed "Oh yeah . . . I can see it now." I could not, in fact, see it now.

On this particular trip, my parents weren't buying it. If I recall correctly, it was an unusually clear, sunny summer day in St. Louis. For whatever reason, the lack of cloud cover made the Arch visible well before we reached the usual spot on the bridge. Sadly, this was what passed for excitement during our family trips.

Over the years I had memorized the spot on the bridge where the Arch typically started to come into view and was prepared to play along as usual. So when someone called out that they had spotted the monument earlier than usual I thought it was a prank. It seemed like a bait and switch to see if I would jump in with my usual "Oh yeah, I can see it, too."

I distinctly remember a shift in the tone of my mom's voice.

"Stop being silly—it's right there," she said as she motioned to what I can only imagine was the easily identifiable edifice. Her tone continued to shift as the fear of impending financial burden crept in.

"You really can't see that?" she pleaded as she continued her interrogation.

I'm still not sure what she suspected my motives were for lying about it. I like to imagine kindergarten-aged me responding with a snarky "Well I've got this great haircut you gave me yourself that looks like the over-sized tip of a circumcised penis, literally every article of clothing I have is some shade of brown or tan and the two pairs of identical Toughskins pants you ordered me from the Sears catalog are in heavy rotation. Busted! I'm really just trying to find a sneaky way of getting my hands on a pair of bulky, thick-lensed glasses to complete the look."

In reality, I'm sure I mumbled some variant of "uh-huh."

Fast forward to a few months later and I did indeed have my very own pair of bulky, thick-lensed glasses to help ensure I looked as goofy on the outside as I felt on the inside. Though I don't remember having any sort of "Praise Jesus! I can see now!" moments. Maybe that was because the elation was outweighed by the fact I now had this foreign apparatus on my face that I apparently had to wear all the time.

What's worse than starting to wear glasses at a ridiculously young age? Accidentally breaking those glasses at recess thanks to an incident involving a large red rubber ball and a distinct lack of dodging on my part.

The moment I felt my nose crunch up against the oversized, blacktop-stained monstrosity that was our class dodgeball, I knew I was in trouble. As my head whiplashed back and the glasses went airborne, all I could think about was my parents losing their shit because they "paid good money for those damn things." Growing up in a working-class family meant there wasn't a rainy-day fund for another pair.

Apparently my brief foray into the seeing world was a one-shot deal because those clunky face-huggers were never replaced. We would eventually revisit the issue of my sketchy eyesight about seven years later when a teacher invited my parents to a special mafia-style "sit down" meeting to discuss my inability to read the chalkboard. *Seven years later.* That's a considerable amount of time spent not being able to make out complex shapes or outlines.

It's no mystery then that for most of my childhood, the idea of swinging a bat with the hopes of hitting some small baseball being hurled my way was more an exercise in luck than skill. I don't think it's an exaggeration to say I struck out at least 90% of the time I was up to bat. The other 10% of the time I was hit by a pitch. Luck of the Irish my ass.

Fortunately, there was an unexpected benefit to being optically-challenged: I couldn't see the look of disappointment on my dad's face up in the stands as I did my trademarked three-strike-shuffle.

My father was never much for outward displays of affection. If we didn't have stacks of photo albums with evidence to the contrary, I'd say he was rarely in the same room with all three of his children at the same time.

To be clear, that's not necessarily a critique. It's hard to give someone something you don't have to give. He was a product of his generation and inherited a legacy of laissez-faire fatherhood. He grew up in the forties, an era where men still mowed their lawn in dress pants. And while I had a relatively warm relationship with my grandfather, I suspect he was much colder to my father. Raising kids was "women's work" and they both fit the traditional stoic Irish American stereotype to a tee.

That's not to say my dad didn't find his own ways to express his love and support, as difficult to recognize as it may have seemed at times. He and I have always been able to find a connection and common ground through sports. Even toward the end of his life when he was sinking deeper and deeper into the same fog of Alzheimer's that swallowed his own father, regaling my dad with stories of the last Cardinals World Series win could—if only for a moment—spark a flicker of light among the haze.

No matter how far the physical or emotional distance was between us, sports were always a safe space. He might not have had much to say about the promotion I'd just received at work or the new relationship I was in, but I could get him talking about who the Rams were playing that weekend. I sustained myself on small talk for decades because it was better than starving. At least it was something.

My father passed away a little less than a year ago. One of the messy truths I'm still trying to work through is the dichotomy of him simultaneously being one of my biggest fans yet also being an emotionally absent father. I can count on one-hand the number of times in my life either of my parents have said "I love you" to me, either out loud or in writing.

One of those rare times was when I was thirteen and had just been busted shoplifting CDs; I'm pretty sure my parents thought it would be a deterrent to my inevitable life of crime. The words wouldn't be articulated again for another handful of years, this time at a religious retreat toward the end of my senior year in high school.

Everyone's parents were supposed to write a letter to their student, congratulating them on whatever sort of spiritual experience was supposed to have happened that week. Somewhere in the directions to parents, it advised them to "tell your child you love them." With all the literary tenacity one might use to fill out a permission slip, my parents included the scripted "I love you" bit as instructed.

Yet my dad supported my athletic endeavors tirelessly. We logged some impressive mileage over the years driving all around the city to games and out-of-state tournaments. Usually, it was just the two of us alone in the car with an awful lot of silence between us. And the occasional Chuck Berry.

While there may not have been much conversation happening, it was still bonding time. Once I entered high school and eventually got my driver's license, those shared miles started to see a significant drop. But he still made it to nearly every game he could. Especially when I was playing football, he never missed a moment.

I know he loved me in the same way I know gravity is a thing—I can feel it but can't really see it or explain how it works exactly. Yet in its absence, I feel untethered and scattered to the wind, drifting aimlessly.

Unfortunately, at the time I didn't have the emotional awareness yet to recognize those athletic outings for what they were: signs of affection. After every football game, as I slowly made my way up the stairs from the field to the locker room, no matter how bruised, battered and bloodied I was, my dad would be there at the top of the stairs waiting for me. Looking back, "good game" and a pat on the back was how he said, "I love you."

As my world started to expand, initially to college a few hours away, then to my first "real" job and eventually multiple moves around the country to cities not named St. Louis, it was harder for my father to maintain that same level of fandom. He was still in my corner—as best he could be—but he no longer understood the "sports" I was playing.

By my mid-twenties, I had already started down a path that was completely foreign to him. And while I desperately wanted to feel his enthusiasm about the fact I had designed my first magazine cover, or pitched a creative idea that won some new business, or simply that I had gone on a date I was really excited about, sharing those milestones with him felt like I was trying to explain nuclear fusion. Somewhere along the way, we lost the shared language sports had given us.

In the last year of his life, as more and more of his mind and memories were lost beneath the crashing waves of dementia, I found myself struggling to find my own words and ways to reach him. Maybe it's my turn to wait for him at the top of the stairs and now that his battle is finally over, greet him with a pat on the back.

Good game, dad.

LOVE AT THE TRUCK STOP

Laurel had Hardy, Batman had Robin and I had Ryan Bosch—at least for the first couple of years I was in high school. The short-but-stout defensive end on our football team was one of the few people who could match my social clumsiness misstep-for-misstep, though that's about where the similarities ended.

He was an extrovert of the highest order with seemingly boundless enthusiasm for nearly everything he encountered, like a puppy just let out of his crate. He dragged me out of my shell pretty aggressively and without my permission—and I loved him for it.

Ryan's overabundance of excitement and general lack of planning were the perfect counterbalance to all the time I spent lost in my own head. He was the epitome of living in the moment.

"Let's do something!" he'd exclaim over the phone.

"Uhhhh . . . maybe. What do you want to do?" I would hesitate, as though the activity needed to pass some sort of review board before being approved.

"I dunno. SOMETHING! I'll pick you up in half an hour."

The lack of detail drove me nuts but before I could think up an excuse he'd be in my driveway honking the horn on his mom's minivan.

Unfortunately, our little buddy flick would be cut short with the news his family was moving to a small farming town in central Illinois at the start of the school year. Realizing we would both be starting our junior year without a partner in crime, it was an easy decision to spend one of our last days as a dynamic duo at Six Flags Over Mid-America, an amusement park about thirty miles outside of St. Louis.

As usual, there was very little planning involved on Ryan's part and before I could start neurotically plotting our path through the park, he was pulling me through the front gate.

Shortly after we made our way through the entrance, we passed the go-karts meant to look like old-timey cars, rounded the corner with the rows of caricature artists and novelty t-shirt booths and headed toward our first roller coaster of the day. That is until we were momentarily delayed by what I can only describe as very courteous catcalling.

From one of the side booths along the main path, we heard a distant "Hey! Hey you guys! You're cute. Come talk to us." Ryan and

I were certain the calls were meant for someone else and looked around for the other actors in what was sure to be a scene straight out of a sitcom. Realizing the only other people in earshot were a family of five and a pack of giggly preteen girls, we braced for impact.

Before we knew it, an overstuffed bouquet of golden-blonde curls was bouncing our way along with the rather sturdy-looking young woman they were attached to. The exuberant lass approaching us wasn't what I would describe as overweight by any means but there was a certain girth to her build that took me a little by surprise. She was nearly as tall as me and about as wide as the left tackle on our football team. Which made it a little confusing when my boy bits started tingling.

Looking back, she was one of the first young women my age I'd met who had what in some circles is described as "a real woman's curves." She was a thick girl—in all the best ways— and at first glance appeared to be hiding two large cantaloupes in her shirt. This combination was all very new to me and I wasn't sure if I wanted to run behind her as she blocked a linebacker or make out with her behind the concession stand. I would have been thrilled with either.

"I'm Jesse," she said in an accent that was an unexpected blend of both country twang and valley girl quirk, offering her hand enthusiastically. Her larger-than-life ponytail had barely stopped swaying before she added "and that's Carlene," shifting her gaze in the direction of the seemingly more-reserved young woman wearing the same blue and red uniform.

Carlene had positioned herself beneath a hanging sign with the words *What's Your Name Mean?* printed in brush-stroke cursive. Her large emerald eyes played peekaboo behind the bangs of her rust-colored hair as she stood solemnly behind the booth's oversized counter like an oracle ready to reveal all.

"Are either of you single?" Jesse asked without hesitation as if she were a used car dealer trying to separate the serious buyers from the lookie-loos. She wasn't wasting her time if we weren't in the market. "I'm not asking for me. I have a man. I'm just asking for my friend over there."

I offered up a shaky "yeah," followed quickly by my friend's more detailed response that—while he too was single—his family was moving at the end of the summer. My competition having gracefully bowed out, I had apparently passed the initial round of interrogation. Jesse grabbed my wrist and walked me over to the booth where her friend had been cautiously evaluating the situation.

"This is Carlene," the bountifully blonde Jesse explained. "She's single, too." Almost on cue, Carlene feigned embarrassment as she playfully slapped her friend on the arm.

"You're such a spaz," Carlene blushed.

"What? You said you wanted to meet people," Jesse replied as she continued the question-and-answer speed round.

While the whole thing felt like a scripted routine they had performed before, my friend and I blissfully played along, just happy to be in the audience.

The conversation stumbled on for a few more minutes, concluding with an exchange of numbers and a promise to come back by the booth before we left the park for the day. Keep in mind, this was long before cell phones became ubiquitous; there was no texting, no storing phone numbers, no calling from the car to say you'd be late because of traffic. It was a scrap of paper, with ten digits written in ink. If any unexpected moisture got in touch with that fragile parchment, you'd be left with little more than illegible smears.

I really don't know how we functioned as a society before smartphones—I haven't memorized a phone number in over a decade, can't read a map to save my life and if someone actually calls my cellphone, I'm expecting either a robocall or catastrophic news.

Digits in hand, Ryan and I excused ourselves and went on our way. But there was no denying what we had just experienced was surely going to be the highlight of the day. The rest of our time in the park would simply be a bonus round.

The triple-loop roller coaster we rode five times in a row, the spinning barrels where I nearly choked to death holding in my own vomit, the electric bumper cars that could barely bump and the endless games of skee-ball that somehow only amounted to a cumulative total of twelve tickets were all just dull, repetitive activities standing between me and the next time I would see Carlene.

Keep in mind, I've said maybe a total of ten words to this girl but I'm already feeling *all* the feels. It was euphoric, if a bit premature. That sensation of going all in immediately would become an unhealthy pattern over the next few decades; I have a tendency to love the idea of the person long before I have any notion of who they actually are.

With great effort, I somehow labored through a day filled with rides, games and general merriment until it was finally time to return to Carlene and Jesse at the *What's Your Name Mean?* booth.

In an attempt to prepare as much banter as I could up front—in case I found myself flailing amid the choppy waters of talking to a girl that had actually shown interest in me—I had a few topics of conversation at the ready. One of my not-so-clever ideas was to ask her what her name meant, considering it was the whole shtick of the booth where they worked.

I'd never met anyone with a name so . . . let's say *rustic*. I assumed the moniker Carlene had its roots all the way back to the beginnings of the trailer park, deep in the hills of the Ozarks or the coal mines of West Virginia. I pictured a father with more children than teeth struggling to come up with a name for his eighth girl, looking out the cracked window of his family's double wide.

"See that there? That car up on them cinders leanin' to the

one side, lookin' like it's 'bout to tip over?" I imagined him saying. "That's what we'll call her. Car-lean."

As it turned out, my premeditated script wouldn't be necessary. As we approached the booth, Carlene had a blank job application in hand that was clearly intended for me.

"We were thinking, since the closing shift guy just quit, and you seem like fun, maybe you'd want to work here?"

She could have just as easily asked if I wanted jumper cables connected to my testicles as I stood ankle-deep in a kiddie pool filled with someone else's urine. The answer was always going to be an enthusiastic *yes*. After a little awkward banter—none of which involved the etymology of names—Ryan and I triumphantly made our way back to the parking lot, noting our epic last day together had been one for the record books.

Working at an amusement park was a great experience I'd never want to do again. While the pros greatly outweighed the cons, I'm the kind of person who doesn't really want to see how the donuts are made. It's not that I don't care, I simply prefer to live in a world where magic exists, even if only in my own mind. It's what made me really good at being Catholic for so many years.

Once I had seen all the hidden employee-only passageways or ridden all the roller coasters after hours for the twenty-second time or had my first week eating nothing but amusement park food, the magic started to fade. And that was kind of a bummer.

Six Flags was as close to a vacation as my family got most years, packing our big red Coleman cooler with soon-to-be soggy sandwiches, multiple cans of Pringles and every flavor of Vess brand soda we could find—including the rare and elusive strawberry— while keeping it all nice and cool with ice packs that I suspect may have been leaking antifreeze.

My dad's extreme frugality meant we couldn't spend any money inside the park, so packing our lunch and coming back out to the car to eat picnic-style on one of the grassy islands in the parking lot was his way of sticking it to the man. By his estimation, entrance to the park for a family of five was already "highway robbery" and they weren't getting "another damn dime out of him."

While working at Six Flags may have taken some of the magic out of those childhood visits, it would prove to be fertile ground for young love. Carlene and I worked different shifts, but there was about an hour of overlap where we could talk and even flirt a little, making the most of the short moments we had between customers. Which seemed to work out fine considering the job itself was pretty mindless, mostly spent framing computer printouts of a majestic mountaintop or lush forest with the name JAMES or ASHLEY in big block letters alongside a mostly made-up origin and meaning. I'm pretty sure every boy's name meant "courageous and strong."

Within the first few weeks of working together, Carlene and I were a couple. In truth, I don't really remember there being much dating before the official "boyfriend / girlfriend" stage. It was pretty straight to the point, appropriately resembling more of a tractor pull that any sort of courting. She was the tractor and I was the . . . whatever they pull. I was happy to be along for the ride and in addition to the emotional high it all brought, there was this new, awesome activity that was now part of my life: making out. And I wanted to do it *all the time.*

I was little more than a strung-out junkie who would do anything for his next fix. I've never done heroin, but I imagine it feels a lot like the first time Carlene stuck her tongue in my mouth during one of our denim-on-denim dry humping sessions. Everything else that existed in the world became a distant second place to that feeling and as we quickly advanced from kissing to heavy petting, to touching places that weren't supposed to be exposed in public, I couldn't get enough. It was like I was always hungry but could never get completely full.

For the record, this is the same reason I'm not allowed around hard drugs.

A few days or so into our blossoming relationship, Carlene asked if I could drive her friend home before my shift started. She would of course accompany us, giving our overactive tongues a little alone time in the employee parking lot when we got back.

She could have just as easily asked me to rob a bank in broad daylight. If there was even a slim chance that afterward she might let me touch one of her boobs, under her shirt but over her bra, my only question would have been what color ski mask she wanted me to wear.

The amusement park where we worked was nestled in the hills of Eureka, Missouri. If St. Louis is the "Gateway to the West" then Eureka was clearly the "Gateway to the Boonies" (or at least it was in the early nineties). Once you passed the Six Flags exit sign headed west on Interstate 44, the towns got much smaller and distinctly more rural.

Not so much agriculturally rural in the sense there were a lot of farms or crops being grown but more the "meth and Monster energy drinks as a major part of the economy" type of rural. These were typically very low-income communities, the kind of towns where Walmart wasn't just the largest employer—it was also the most popular place for social gatherings.

When Carlene told me we would be dropping her friend off four highway exits past Six Flags, I got a little anxious. When she proceeded to explain her own family lived another two exits past that, I was full-on freaking out. We were undoubtedly headed "in country."

∾

While driving down the crooked country roads it occurred to me for the first time that I was the "rich kid" in this scenario. Judging by

Carlene's reaction when I mentioned I lived in the suburbs of West St. Louis County, I may as well have said I lived in Beverly Hills. It was a complete role reversal for me; I was used to playing the part of the disadvantaged underdog with a chip on his shoulder.

I complained about my family's small, crowded ranch house compared to the newly-built two-story homes most of my classmates lived in and felt a little ashamed of the fact I drove an older, used car instead of a brand-new Eddie Bauer Ford Explorer. But to Carlene, the fact I had my own car was a rare luxury and she had classmates who literally lived in a trailer park—which, for the record, was actually a lot nicer than what they show on TV. I thought it pretty much looked like any other blue-collar neighborhood.

The perspective was humbling. It also shed light on how little I cared about material things or social status when looking for a partner. If you're cute and like to make out with me, I don't care if you live in a cardboard box.

I'd been driving for less than a year and this was long before GPS was as widely available as it is today, so the winding roads had me on edge. My sweaty palms felt cold and slippery as they gripped the wheel while Carlene called out turn-by-turn directions from the passenger seat. Thankfully, we arrived safely at her friend's house, dropped her off and started on our way back to Six Flags.

As the country roads started to fade in my rearview mirror, I began to feel a little more at ease. Carlene wanted me to take the route through "town" on the way back so she could show me around and considering there was the prospect of tongue wrestling in my very near future, *no* wasn't really in my vocabulary.

When we approached a four-way stop at the bottom of the hill just outside of town, I paused for what I thought was at least three seconds. In truth, Carlene putting her hand on my upper thigh made my pulse quicken significantly and it may have distorted my perception of time and space. As I pulled out into the intersection, we were almost immediately t-boned by a speeding pickup truck.

All I remember is hearing the deafening crunch of metal on metal as my car spun 180°, finally coming to a halt in the opposite lane facing oncoming traffic. Miraculously, no one suffered any major injuries other than a few scrapes and bruises. My car wasn't so lucky—it had been crumpled up like discarded aluminum foil.

Even now, thinking about that scene gives me goosebumps. Had I pulled out into the intersection a second slower, it would have been the driver-side door that was crushed instead of the now-empty backseat and this story would have a very different ending.

As the police arrived to file the report, the shock and adrenaline slowly started to wear off. Then I noticed the paramedics examining Carlene. Apparently during the crash, a small piece of glass had gotten in her eye and it was now noticeably bloodshot and starting to swell. Thankfully, she didn't need to go to the hospital, but she would need to explain what happened to her parents. And that was going to be a problem.

Carlene was fifteen at the time (a year younger than me) and her parents had a strict rule that she wasn't allowed to ride in anyone's car but their own. Being fairly comfortable dismissing most of my own parents' rules, I had a hard time understanding why she was more upset about the consequences of her disobedience than the near-fatal accident.

Looking back, I can definitely understand her parents concern, especially considering they were trying to prevent exactly what had happened. My time spent driving in suburbia was far from treacherous, mostly spent going 25 mph through residential neighborhoods with the occasional leisurely jaunt on the highway.

Where Carlene lived, the roads were far more dangerous, poorly lit and even more poorly managed and the drivers seemed to consider the speed limit a bare minimum due to the virtually non-existent police presence. Automobile fatalities among teenagers were especially high.

For the rest of the summer, most of my time spent with Carlene continued to be limited to within the friendly confines of the amusement park where we worked. And that was just fine by me— she was my first everything, so there was no baseline for what "normal" dating was supposed to look like. But with the start of the school year looming on the horizon, our relationship was about to take a bizarre turn.

After Six Flags closed for the season, Carlene got a part-time job on the weekends at Mr. Fuel, the truck stop down the road from where she lived. Her mother had worked there for years and was a local legend with the truckers that would pass through on their way out west.

A short, plump woman with rosy red cheeks and a ponytail down to her caboose, Carlene's mom was an outgoing, outspoken country girl through and through. A warm woman, she made me feel at ease from the first time I met her. She would routinely be the one picking up Carlene from Six Flags over the summer, giving me the chance to get to know her in five-minute intervals.

She drove a baby blue, partially-rusted-out Suburban that looked like it could seat fourteen people comfortably, always had a half-smoked Marlboro red cigarette dangling from her lips along with a liter of Mt. Dew at the ready and smiled more frequently than any other adult I had ever met.

Door-to-door it was over an hour drive from my house to Carlene's, so once school started things got complicated. Since she wasn't allowed to drive in my car, traditional dates were out of the question. And she wasn't allowed "in the city" by herself, which is what her family called any place with a population of more than 10,000 people.

The only option was hanging out at her house, so most of our "dates" included a chaperone of some sort, whether it was her mother or her older sister. Her dad worked nights and occasional weekends on the assembly line at the local Dodge plant and I had football games ever Friday night, so it was a few months into the school year before my path crossed her father's for the first time.

Back in high school I thought I was a pretty tough dude that didn't scare very easily. (I also thought silly things like that mattered.) I was a starting linebacker on the varsity football team and thanks to the ever-present chip on my shoulder, rarely walked away from an opportunity to exchange a few punches when prompted.

Then I met Carlene's dad and discovered the true meaning of the word *intimidation*. The polar opposite of his wife, he was thickly bearded with a pock-marked face and unusually large hands that seemed like they were calloused from birth. He looked like a Bruce Springsteen song.

While Carlene's dad wasn't a particularly large man in stature, there was a harshness in him that transcended his physical frame. He rarely spoke but when he did, his raspy tone demanded attention. Not in the sense that he had a booming voice that overpowered the room but more because he spoke so quietly you had to really concentrate to hear what he was saying, which somehow always seemed to give him the advantage.

Carlene's mom on the other hand was a bird that was always chirping, so you could miss entire sentences and still get the gist of what she was saying. But when her husband spoke, each word required you stop what you were doing and listen. He was not a man to be trifled with.

Carlene and I were one of those silly, puppy-love-fueled couples that embarrassingly celebrated every little anniversary. Two weeks, one month, three months—all with cards and gifts and proclamations of eternal love. It was pretty gross.

As we approached our six-month anniversary, we might as well have been planning our wedding. But because the big day happened to be in the middle of the week, scheduling our romantic evening was a little complicated with school the next day and the hour-long drive between us. Heaven forbid we wait until the weekend to celebrate; that would be our six-month-and-three-day anniversary. Definitely not the same thing.

For better or worse, my parents had all but conceded any control of me at this point. While they had rules for my older sister so strict she may as well had been living in a nunnery, my stubbornness had worn them down to the point where I was mostly left to my own devices.

My dad's point of view was that I couldn't get pregnant so what harm could it do, and my mom was working nights at a nursing home, mostly to avoid my father. Neither of them were going to be featured on the cover of *Parenting* magazine anytime soon.

The big night comes and Carlene says she has a special surprise for me. She and her mother had prepared a romantic dinner for us, complete with tablecloths and candlelight. But the real surprise was that—unbeknownst to her father who was working his usual night shift—her mother had planned to give us the house to ourselves for a few hours while she visited with a neighbor down the street.

At the time, it felt like the ultimate wingman move and I loved her mom for it. But I think it's closer to the truth to say that if it had been fifty years or so earlier, Carlene's mom would have married her off as a child bride with little hesitation. Fifteen through seventeen are prime dating years in the trailer park and I think her mom was genuinely convinced the two of us would "get hitched" as soon as we could. If Carlene had a bun in the oven, all the better.

I was sixteen and still a virgin at this point. Truth be told, Carlene had pretty much been my first everything, from French kissing to touching naughty bits. She, however, was not a virgin and I was most certainly not her first anything.

Before the ghosts of our tight-assed Puritanical forefathers start rolling over in their graves or the Catholics start lining up to throw stones, I'm not saying she was promiscuous. She wasn't— though we could all probably stand to tone down the slut shaming considerably. She was a sweet girl with a big heart that she shared with people readily.

She was also very comfortable initiating physical intimacy, which was one of the reasons we worked so well together. Not only did I gladly let her take the lead, I preferred it. If things had progressed all on my terms, we'd probably never have graduated from holding hands; I couldn't quite shake the feeling that Jesus was watching and keeping score like some divine voyeur.

After that evening, we *knew one another* in the biblical sense. And I have to say, all in all, there are a lot worse ways to lose your virginity. If simply making out felt like heroin, this carnal cocktail was on a whole other level, more akin to going on a five-day bender through Vegas with Hunter S. Thompson. Unfortunately, it would be a rare treat considering we were never allowed to leave the house together and any time spent in her room was with the door open and a parent down the hall.

A few months later, her family invited me over to celebrate New Year's Eve. Her parents and their fellow hard-working, hard-drinking friends were an energetic, rowdy bunch known to tie one on into the wee hours of the morning. Which suited Carlene and I just fine. While the festivities were raging in the backyard, we were having our own little two-person party inside the house, rotating between cuddling, making out and slow dancing to corny Reba McEntire songs.

At some point shortly after midnight, her more-cheery-than-usual mother informed me that it was too dangerous for me to drive all the way home and that I would be staying the night with them. It was a kind gesture that had my best interests at heart and considering she was relaying information more than asking for my thoughts on the matter, I proceeded to call home and let my dad in on our plans.

As you might imagine, there was little need for convincing but to seal the deal I asked Carlene's now nearly-slurring mother to chime in. Both sides being satisfied with the arrangement, we considered it a done deal.

Carlene proceeded to set up a makeshift bed for me on the couch, brought me some toiletries and said goodnight, though her tone and hand placement under my gym shorts implied it was temporary and that I would be getting a surprise visitor later that night.

A few minutes went by before I heard much heavier footsteps down the hallway. As the steps got louder, their owner turned the corner into the living room. There was her father, shotgun in hand.

For what it's worth, to this day I've never so much as held a real gun, let alone fired one. I've never had any kind of interest in firearms and don't see that changing anytime in the near future. None of that would matter, of course, because her dad was not there to talk about the joys of gun ownership.

Clearly tipsy—but thankfully not aiming the shotgun in my

direction—he spoke a little louder than usual, ensuring each word hit its mark.

"I'm allowing you to stay in my home. Don't break that trust and make me regret it," he snarled.

"Uhhhh . . . no sir," the words dribbled out of my shaking lips.

"Your place is on that couch, understand? No funny business," he warned me, unknowingly contradicting his daughter's earlier innuendo. But I was on *Team No Funny Business* all the way.

"Yes, sir," I responded adamantly, nearly giving him a salute in the process.

Satisfied with my earnest reply, Carlene's father retired to his bedroom. Not only did I have no interest in ever touching his daughter again, but I was now seriously considering taking up a monastic calling and spending the rest of my days swearing off all contact with the outside world.

While his methods left something to be desired—what with the whole implied homicide and all—you couldn't argue with the results. Unfortunately, these biological machines we're stuck in are funny things and not all of my gears and widgets were in complete agreement about the planned celibacy.

Sure enough, a few hours later, my night visitor was gently nudging me to wake from my slumber. In what was barely more than a whisper, I rebuked Carlene's advances, primarily citing the fear of death. Undeterred, she decided to speak to the one part of my body that was still protesting the entire situation. In one smooth motion, she slid her hand under the blanket and woke up the rest of me.

It was in that moment that I realized my body was not to be trusted. Despite my brain desperately trying to slam on the breaks, the rest of me completely disregarded the command. It was go time.

While no shots were fired that night—at least not from her father's shotgun—I still woke up feeling betrayed. Not by Carlene but by my own hormones. In my mind, they had nearly gotten me killed. My years and years of Catholic school had instilled an intense fear of premarital sex and I had been warned time and again of the risk, but this was ridiculous.

Yet despite our late-night rendezvous, I must have passed the test because these sleepovers became a regular occurrence, albeit with a few modifications. Someone must have known something was up because the new arrangement was that I was to sleep in Carlene's room while she would sleep on the floor in her parent's bedroom—with them—with the door locked.

This Fort Knox situation was mostly successful in halting any midnight make out sessions but it certainly didn't completely stop us from bumping uglies. We simply got more creative about where and when we were intimate. Where there's a teenage boy with a rock-hard erection, there's a way.

This sleepover routine continued nearly every weekend for the next three months or so, creating a really unusual dynamic where it felt like I lived with Carlene's family on the weekends. She would get up to work at the truck stop on Saturday morning and I would keep myself busy playing games on her computer.

Keep in mind, I was a junior in high school and this was my first-ever girlfriend. Over the course of less than a year, I went from being a shy, inexperienced Catholic schoolboy to essentially a live-in partner, complete with extra clothes and a toothbrush stashed at her place.

Eventually the velocity of it all caught up with me and I knew I had to end things. Breaking up with someone was one more thing I'd never had to do before and just like the romance, it would be a pretty intense experience for my inaugural attempt.

I don't remember all the specifics of the break-up but I'll certainly never forget the results. Carlene was devastated and so were her parents. Everyone was hearing wedding bells and I had just set the church on fire. But somewhere deep inside, I knew the past year's trip to redneck crazytown needed to be temporary or I was at risk of becoming a permanent resident.

In what was the classic overly-dramatic teenage break-up trifecta, Carlene threatened to kill herself, faked a pregnancy scare and immediately started sleeping with one of her closest guy friends. Like a broken bone that never quite heals right and always gets a little twitchy when rain is on the way, the ending of the relationship warped my perception of break-ups. It was all just way too much.

At the start of my senior year a classmate offered to introduce me to her best friend who attended one of the local Catholic all-girls schools near where we lived. And that was just the right medicine to heal the heaviness of the previous year—a nice, calm, mostly reserved Catholic girl that I would occasionally spend a few hours with on a Saturday night, doing little more than cuddling and occasionally making out—at a slow and comfortably Catholic pace that Jesus would have been proud of.

My second attempt at a high school relationship was a pleasantly uneventful experience—at least by the truck stop standards I had come to know—and we ended up dating for most of the year. We parted ways somewhat amicably as I left for college in the fall, at which point I pledged to permanently give up all forms of roller coasters, emotional or otherwise.

It wasn't a pledge I was able to keep for very long.

. . . AND POETRY FOR ALL

I've always found sanctuary in libraries. Maybe it's the quiet, or the feeling of getting lost in the stacks, or just the fact I can be alone and comfortably adrift in my own mind with thousands of new adventures at my fingertips. Especially during my preteen years, the library was a safe haven where I could openly embrace and hone my own developing, individual tastes. It was the freedom of unassigned learning.

I could poke around in almost any topic at will, moving on as soon as I lost interest, within minutes flowing from a biography of Mohamed Ali to a book on drawing monsters to a witty play by Oscar Wilde. And I could do it all far from the judging eyes of others; if I wanted to spend an hour re-reading a *Choose Your Own Adventure* book over and over until I had exhausted all the possibilities, no one was going to stop me.

While the books were a special treat, they were really just the appetizer. The rows and rows of music available to check out were the main entrée and I couldn't wait to dig in. Featured prominently in the center of the library, behind the reference cards, were modified steel magazine racks with square, bucketed shelves that held about ten cassettes each, loosely categorized by genre, then alphabetically. The tapes were stored in blue plastic sleeves with the cover of the album tucked into a clear pocket on the front like a custom name tag.

Because there was no way to preview the music on the spot and I could only check out five cassette tapes at a time, there was a lot of experimentation involved. Looking back, it reminds me of the Zen Buddhist concept *Shoshin* that describes the "beginner's mind" as a state of openness and possibility without expectation, especially as it relates to learning new things. That feels like a perfect description of my musical exploration at the library. I was looking-yet-not-looking for the band or album that would be my next favorite.

Typically, I would start by searching for musicians I already knew that had an extensive catalog beyond what I was familiar with. The deeper the cuts the better, especially considering unless I owned the album or borrowed it from a friend, the only songs I could hear were the singles on the radio or MTV.

Since there wasn't even an internet at the time, let alone phones that could stream music instantly, my access to full albums was pretty limited. While I love the convenience of listening to music today, part of me misses the risk / reward of taking a chance on an artist I was completely unfamiliar with, like some sort of album archaeologist unearthing a long-buried treasure.

If I couldn't find musicians I knew, I would pick based on the album cover. While not the most scientific method, it allowed for some really wonderful accidental discoveries early on. I stumbled across bands like The Smiths, Violent Femmes, Rush and even Nick Drake based on little more than what I thought was cool artwork. While this method didn't always work—I'm looking at you, Meatloaf—it was a great way to discover music I might not have otherwise been exposed to and all it required was a library card and a little trial and error.

Music was also my gateway drug into poetry. Growing up, most of the poems I had been exposed to at school were variations of squishy, overly sentimental odes to flowers or trees or someone's betrothed, whatever that meant. They may as well have been written in Latin. I was enthusiastically uninterested. And I definitely didn't consider the lyrics to the songs I loved poetry. Music was cool, poetry was lame. It seemed pretty cut and dry. Until it wasn't.

During one my routine library visits when I was around thirteen years old, after a somewhat unfruitful search for new music, I spotted one of the carts used to return items to the shelves out in the open, full of fresh loot and clearly unattended. Having yet to reach my five-cassette limit, I approached the cart with all the desperation of the last few singles in a bar after last call but before the lights go on. I was taking all five of my allotted tapes home, even if it meant swallowing my pride and significantly lowering my standards.

Upon further investigation, I was pleasantly surprised to find a cassette of The Doors *Strange Days* nestled between a few Barbara Streisand records and a compilation of Sonny and Cher's greatest hits. While I was loosely familiar with The Doors from the radio, I'd never listened to an entire album so I jumped at the chance to check it out. This was a few years before Oliver Stone's award-winning biopic, so Jim Morrison's showmanship, excess and eccentric nature was still mostly a mystery to me.

After collecting my prize, something else on the cart caught my eye. Stashed away on the bottom shelf was a book with Jim Morrison's name in big, bold print. Assuming it was a biography of the legendary front man, I figured I'd casually flip through a few of the pages before it was returned to its home in the stacks.

I soon discovered it was *The Lords and New Creatures*, a collection of original poetry written by Jim Morrison. I cracked open the tome expecting to find little more than lyrics without music. Twenty minutes later, I was still standing in the exact same spot, motionless except for the turning of pages.

Surely this didn't count as poetry, right? It was weird, and dark, and at times nonsensical, and absolutely fascinating. I thought it was undeniably, unequivocally cool.

While re-reading the collection as an adult was a distinctly less-enlightening experience—it felt more pompous and pretentious to me than powerful or poignant—as an adolescent I was absolutely in awe. While I really didn't "get it," I desperately wanted to.

That was my 101-level introduction to the "other" kinds of poetry and I was eager to sign up for more. But I had no idea where to begin and was far too embarrassed about my newly discovered interest to ask for anyone's help, including the librarians. My exploration into poetry was a closely-guarded secret—I would stash the books under my bed like I was hiding a stack of *Playboys* or a pack of cigarettes. I was a tough guy and a jock. Expressing any kind of interest in poetry was very much off-brand.

Not really sure how to find more of these exotic literary works, I took a similar approach to how I looked for music. I started randomly checking out books of poetry based on little more than the cover design and the author's name.

Just like my regular searches through the racks of cassette tapes, the randomness of just grabbing a book of poetry from the shelves led me down some interesting paths, including my accidental introduction to a poet whose work still deeply resonates with me today: e.e. cummings.

He wrote poetry the way jazz sounds, breaking all the rules, using capitalization and punctuation however he pleased and improvising at will. There was also a visual element to his poetry that I was instantly fascinated by; the way the words were laid out on the page was just as much part of the experience as what they were saying.

It was around this time that my parents brought home our family's first electronic word processor. The technological marvel could easily be mistaken for a nicer, modern electric typewriter at first glance if it weren't for the small gray screen that was no bigger than today's smartphones. The unit had a tiny computer processor inside that allowed you to type out entire paragraphs before a single drop of ink hit the page. You could edit, delete, copy, paste and even save onto a 3.5" floppy disk. Compared to writing on a typewriter, it was a pretty monumental breakthrough.

Like a lot of the technology of the era, it seemed revolutionary when it came out. Over time, however, it proved to be a temporary solution; it wasn't *the thing*, it was the thing right before *the thing*. Personal computers were still a handful of years away from taking up a permanent residence in most homes and typewriters were an antiquated relic of the past.

That feels like a telling reflection of my generation. We're not the Baby Boomers who built—and then subsequently broke—everything. We're not the Millennials who get blamed for everything yet will ultimately be the ones fixing it all. My generation is stuck somewhere in the middle of this tug-of-war trying to keep both sides from killing one another. While we've been labeled Generation X, it seems like a more fitting title would be The In-Between Generation.

This new way of writing where I could easily edit on-screen and save to a disk had an unexpectedly positive influence on my earliest creative development; it meant I could pretend I was a professional.

I've always had horrible penmanship that looks like I'm writing with a crayon stuck between my toes. It's not unusual for me to take notes that even I can't decipher when I go back to read them later. As a result, my earliest attempts at creative writing visually looked to me like something written by an amateur, regardless of the message or word choice. Every poem I wrote looked like the hastily scribbled diary entries of a small child. But now with this shiny new electronic device, I could fake it. Thanks to my good friend Times New Roman, even my earliest ramblings at least *looked* professional.

Like a lot of young artists, I started learning my craft by being a knock-off, made-in-China version of the writers I admired. In the same way an illustrator might learn their craft from tracing over the sketches of their favorite artists, I was tracing words.

For me, more often than not that meant trying to imitate e.e. cummings. I'd space out the letters of certain words for effect, have weird line breaks for no real reason other than to make the stanza "look cool," obnoxiously write every line in lowercase and use lots of fancy, clever words despite the fact I didn't have the slightest idea what they meant.

Reading my earliest writing was like having a conversation at a dinner party with someone who keeps name-dropping B-list celebrities with the hopes of sounding important. "You know, I once went water skiing with the lead singer of Smash Mouth" was the equivalent of me using words like *feign* or *macabre* in my poetry. I didn't really know what they meant and was shamelessly trying to sound intelligent. It usually had the opposite effect.

Eventually, I started to fill up my floppy disks with semi-original poetry. It was original in the sense that I wrote it but followed the standard mopey teenager / tormented soul template populated with little more than overly dramatic musings and copycat ideas. But I was writing fairly frequently and quickly fell in love with the process. And once every lunar cycle, I'd come up with an original line that wasn't complete dribble. I was very slowly starting to learn the craft, though still very much in secret.

By the time the summer before my freshman year of high school rolled around, I had a stack of disks filled with my poems and occasional prose. Of the fifty or so pieces I had written, two or three were almost average, so I was starting to think about how I might share my apparent emerging genius with the world.

The perfect opportunity arose on a typically humid St. Louis summer evening, the kind of night where the air was thick enough to taste and the mosquitoes outnumbered the human population two-to-one.

The kids who I had just graduated junior high with were getting together for what was generously described as a "party." In the eight years I had spent with these people, there had never once been any sort of class-wide co-ed social activity, so it was bound to be about as interesting as watching paint dry. And you could tell we all viewed the evening as a sort of practice round for what we imagined would be our active social calendars once we reached high school. It was a bit premature though well-intended.

This little gathering of overly familiar faces seemed like a perfectly safe opportunity to share some of the things I'd written. We all grew up together, very few of us were attending the same high schools in the fall and there was all the sexual chemistry you might expect to find at a convention of castrated monks.

But I wasn't ready to share my writing quite so directly, so I printed out three of my favorite original poems along with the lyrics to songs from Metallica's . . . *And Justice For All* album, passing them off as my own writing. If you're unfamiliar with the heavy metal band's earlier work, the songs I pilfered lyrics from had titles like *To Live is To Die, Harvester of Sorrow* and *The Frayed Ends of Sanity.*

As you might imagine, there were very few thematic similarities to my own poetry. But I wanted to throw people off the scent and quickly shake any preconceived notions of my poetry being about puppies, flowers or rainbows. I was tackling heavy, dark issues. Or so I thought.

In truth, I over-steered considerably with the lyrics I blatantly plagiarized. The most common reaction from my classmates was concern for my mental health. As it turns out, lyrics like "growing conspiracy / myself is after me" or "my life suffocates / planting seeds of hate" didn't play particularly well at a party filled with fourteen-year-old Catholic school students.

As misguided as it was, the experience was a big step toward "coming out" as a writer, poet and storyteller. I was using the training wheels of someone else's words while I gained the courage and momentum to find my own. In many ways, it was the start of *this* . . . and everything after.

C.W. Emge was born and raised in St. Louis, Missouri and currently lives in Portland, Oregon. He is an author, essayist, poet and artist.

For more original stories, visit

www.cwemge.com

@CW_Emge